EMILE

→ EMILE ZOLA

An Introductory Study of his Novels

by

ANGUS WILSON

New York

WILLIAM MORROW & COMPANY

Manufactured in the United States of America

FOR VIVA KING

CONTENTS

Chapter I

EARLY LIFE

Birth – his father – his mother – background of early
years – education – friendships – literary enthusiasms –
visual, psychological and social effects of early years on
his later work – ambivalent attitude to Aix – Paris –
his relations with Cézanne – failure and near starvation –
Docks – reading – liaison with prostitute – Hachette –
Contes à Ninon – *La Confession de Claude* – Journalism –
Defence of Impressionists – Importance of their works
to Zola – Alexandrine Meley – the 'triangle situation' –
Madeleine Férat – *Thérèse Raquin* – Move to Right Bank –
Social and literary position at outbreak of Franco-
Prussian War – Career in War.

T HE form in which an artist's creative impulses
are ultimately expressed is frequently moulded by
the stresses placed upon his emotions in childhood
and early adolescence; stresses produced by the gradual
realization of the dreadful gulf that lies between his fantasy world, often protected and nurtured by parental
affection, and the vast, uncomforting desert of the
society in which he must live. Artistic creation, it would
seem, represents such fragments of this fantasy world
as he is able to retain and to impose upon society. Every
accident of Émile Zola's birth and upbringing enriched
his artistic growth by heightening this painful contrast
and sharpening the adolescent struggle to retain the
visions of childhood. Though he was forced by poverty

and hardship to renounce these dreams, he ultimately transformed them into a nightmare world which, by his imaginative force and his brilliant analysis of those evils which contemporary society strove to forget, amply avenged him for his disillusionment by forcing from that society the success and recognition his pride demanded. There were other crises and frustrations in his later life which affected the shape of his work and prolonged this artistic conflict beyond the point where success might have produced a false resolution; but the basic struggle and its symbolic expression, which give to the Rougon-Macquart novels their vitality and greatness, are the inheritance of his earliest years, the more deeply significant, perhaps, because unlike so many great novelists, he seldom worked them out in direct reminiscence of his childhood.

Émile Zola was born on April 2nd 1840 in the Rue St.-Joseph, a street situated in the market quarter of Paris. His father François Zola, of Greco-Italian origin, had passed a somewhat chequered early career in the army, and certain doubtful events of this period were later used to discomfort his son at the time of the Dreyfus incident. He was, however, an imaginative and competent engineer, who, after various unsuccessful attempts to interest Louis Philippe's ministers in ambitious projects, had been entrusted with the important task of canalizing the water supply of Aix-en-Provence, a town which was annually threatened by serious drought. In 1839 he visited Paris in order to gain the interest of Thiers, who was himself a native of Aix. Here he met the Auberts, a family of upper peasant origin from Dourdon in the Ile-de-France, and shortly afterwards married their daughter, Émilie. Émile Édouard Charles Antoine, as he was christened, was their only child. In 1842 the family returned to Aix, where building on the canal was due to begin; here they occupied a pleasant house with a rambling garden in the Impasse Sylvacanne, in the new middle-class quarter of the old Romano-medieval town which Émile Zola was to make the home of Pierre and Félicité, the founders of the Rougon fortune. In 1846 Monsieur and Madame Zola visited Marseilles on business and there, in a hotel, François Zola contracted pleurisy and died at the age of fifty-one. His death meant a sudden reversal of the family fortune against which his widow and her parents were to fight a losing battle throughout Émile's childhood.

It is difficult to estimate the significance of his father's memory in Zola's life. Although he showed persistent interest during his early manhood in the recognition of his father's work for Aix, the tone of his letters to his friends Roux and Baille on the subject suggests that he saw this recognition as a move in his own revenge upon the town for his humiliation there as a child, rather than as any realisation of a personal belief in his father's merited glory. It was not his father's near success, which was, after all, prevented not by personal defects but by death, that seems to have impressed Zola, but the fact of his father's failure, by which his son had directly suffered as a child. Émile's ambition and will to power, almost the most important elements in his genius, would seem to have derived not from rivalry of his father's achievements but from determination to avoid his lack of success. This view of his father must presumably have come from his mother. The recapitulation by Hélène Mouret in *Une Page d'Amour* of her painful experience as a stranger in a Paris hotel with her dying husband suggests the sort of vivid narrative of her own experiences in Marseilles to which Madame François Zola probably treated her son in his childhood. If this identification is correct, Madame Zola emerges as a woman speaking of her dead husband in tones of worship, but dramatically heightening those moments of her own sacrifice which would ultimately tilt the balance of her son's divided devotion. Now, of course, she had the field to herself.

Both the internal evidence of the novels and the position she occupied in her son's later domestic arrangements show clearly the ascendancy that she gained over his emotions, an ascendancy which his marriage did not break, and which lasted, despite quarrels, until her death in 1880, an event which perhaps more nearly destroyed his precarious mental balance than any other in his life. Like every other deep attachment in the life of a man so divided as Zola, it was, of course, ambivalent, and if his mother was to be honoured in Hélène Mouret, her possessive love of her son is described more equivocally in the character of Madame Chanteau in *La Joie de Vivre* and she may even have unconsciously provided some of the material for the terrifying figure of Félicité Rougon, whose energetic ambition strikes like a brutal whip across so many of the Rougon-Macquart novels, and who finally, in *Le Docteur Pascal* destroys, in her worldly ambition, the very things that her son – an acknowledged self-portrait – held most dear.

The seeds of these intense, ambivalent emotions had perfect forcing ground in the close, shut-in atmosphere of his childhood home. Moving to ever poorer quarters of Aix, Madame Zola, with the assistance of her equally energetic, determined mother, fought with courage against her environment. The hatred of these northern French peasant women must indeed have been bitter towards their more prosperous Provençal bourgeois neighbours, who were witnesses of their degradation, but their greatest loathing must have been reserved for the local poor to whose level, despite the cruel sacrifice of their cherished possessions, they were inevitably sinking. Émile's nerves, one suspects, must have been torn to pieces by appeals to his pride not to mix with the local children, by fierce affectionate belief in his future powers to raise the family fortunes, and by a joyless emphasis upon virtue, education and saving as the proud marks that distinguished his home from the hovels of the neighbouring poor.

If his affection and ambitions were aroused by such exhortations, he must nevertheless have found relief in the long happy rambles with his school friend Marius Roux among the surrounding hills. The picture of Aix society in the Rougon-Macquart novels shows that he despised and hated his Provençal neighbours as much as his mother could have hoped for. Nevertheless he acquired a love of the bright colours and sweet scents of the Provençal countryside, of the white, rocky hills, the vineyards, the twisted fig-trees, and the lush overgrown estates that must have made his home seem all the more grim. It is this early response to a countryside of strongly contrasted sunlight and shadow that awoke his sharp visual sense to the pervasiveness of light throughout the external world, an appreciation of atmospheric conditions that was even more keenly aroused by the subtle light of the Seine countryside, giving him a direct bond of sympathy with the work of the Impressionist painters who so deeply influenced his writing. In particular such half-wild estates and gardens as the eighteenth-century Parc du Château de Gallice must have appealed to the social dreams carefully nurtured by his family, and to his romantic imagination which was now being awakened by a diet of Hugo, Lamartine and Vigny: it is no wonder that the Parc later formed the model for the natural paradise of Paradou in *La Faute de l'Abbé Mouret*.

Meanwhile his education was being pushed ahead by his mother. After the Coup d'État of 1851 her hopes of getting money from the canal scheme became slight, for Thiers, on whom she relied, belonged to the fallen régime. By compounding her claims in return for a small sum, however, and moving to a poorer house, Madame Zola was able to send Émile to the local high school — the Collège Bourbon. He was older than most of the boys in his class, and although he obtained many first and second prizes, the standard cannot have been very high, for among his distinctions were some in Latin of which he later disclaimed knowledge, and in English, although he did not read Shakespeare in the original and found speaking very difficult when he later came to England as an exile. Some critics of Zola, particularly Léon Daudet, made much of his lack of education, but this is hardly a serious charge against an imaginative novelist of the nineteenth century. His educational standard would seem to have been a little better than that of Charles Dickens, whose naïve enthusiasm for Buckle and the Positivists in his later life parallels Zola's uncritical adaptation of the theories of Darwin and Claude Bernard to the realm of literature. At seventeen he opted to transfer to the science side, but his residence at the school was soon after brought to an end through family poverty. The most important aspect of his schooldays lay in his close friendship with Baille and Paul Cézanne. Equal enthusiasts for the countryside, the three youths passed whole days on expeditions in which they read aloud the works of their beloved Hugo, and Lamartine, and discovered the charms of Musset; they also composed poems, plays and stories. Only one of these youthful works of Zola was to appear in his first published stories — *La Fée amoureuse* in the *Contes à Ninon*.

By 1857 Madame Zola and her parents had moved to a two-roomed workman's cottage in the Rue Mazarine, and here the indomitable Madame Aubert died, worn out by hard work and worry. The family fortunes were so precarious that Madame Zola decided to go to Paris to seek help from friends, and a week later she summoned Émile to follow her, bringing his grandfather with him. By favour of a friend of the family, Émile obtained a place on the science side at the Lycée Saint-Louis. His health and nervous system had been overtaxed and he soon fell gravely ill with a fever. It seems likely that in the pleasant half-dreams of his convalescence he found an escape from the horrors of reality. This may well have been the source of his almost negative reaction to life in the next few years which contrasts so strangely with his later aggressive will to succeed. At any rate the impact of this illness upon his imagination provides the basis of much of his later hypochondria, and of the disproportionate role that sickbeds play in his novels, culminating in the pathological atmosphere of *Joie de Vivre*.

He soon after failed to secure his diploma in Paris, where his proficiency in the sciences was offset by his historical ignorance — a lifelong trait — for in the oral he placed Charlemagne in the fifteenth century. A second attempt at Marseilles was equally unsuccessful. He found himself, therefore, at the age of seventeen with no hope of continuing his education, and no qualifications to secure employment in the social class towards which all Madame Zola's sacrifices had been bent.

Unconsciously, however, these apparently pointless years had seen the creation of further powerful neurotic conflicts which were to find their outlet in the twenty novels of the Rougon-Macquart. He had acquired an emotional hostility to society, which, when he recovered from a period of youthful, idealistic rejection of existence, was to supply the overwhelming force of his work and combine with his acute observation and analytical powers to make one of the greatest series of social novels ever written. The concentration of his childhood happiness upon a bright and colourful countryside had made him exceptionally responsive both to sight and smell, and this almost pathologically nervous sensitivity infused his work with an atmospheric tension which removes it from the field of social comment to a realism, at once exact and impressionistic, and unique in literature. His long apprenticeship to the romantic writers and his youthful efforts to succeed as a poet bequeathed to his novels a lyricism of imagination, which his advancing technical powers eventually fused into the body of his work, so that in his greatest novels there is a complete unity of personal fantasy and social observation that forces his readers to accept his view of the world as the objectively real one. Finally, his convictions of the evil foundations of society, the product of the equivocal social position of his family and his own resulting personal isolation, had found a particular symbol in sexual promiscuity. It was portrayed as the central cause of failure, corruption, decay and futility for all classes of society in his novels. The uninhibited outdoor love-making, which appears to have marked the Provençal peasantry of his childhood environment, was probably a source of excitement and envy to his growing desires, enmeshed as they were in his dependence upon his mother's affections, and a shock to his Hugo-fed romantic ideals, centred, as we shall see later, on a personal fantasy. It was probably also the target for his family's social reprobation and class-conscious moralising. If we can judge from the novels about Plassans, as he called Aix, Zola was not long in seeing an equal promiscuity, though a more hypocritical one, in the bourgeois society of that town. However distorted this rejection of physical sexuality with its curious underlying sensual flavour may appear, it gave an intensity and a continuity to all his work at a far deeper level than any of the intellectual systems by which he later attempted to explain it. With this psychological equipment, rather than with any educational diplomas or degrees, he was to conquer Paris and eventually the whole reading world of the later nineteenth century.

Émile, then, had failed his mother, and for the next two and a half years he was to underline this fact by obstinately clinging to the dream world of his boyhood. Only the absolute destitution and personal misery, resulting from his 'bohemian' rejection of respectable society in these years, forced him eventually to return to the concepts of social ambition and power which her teaching represented. We can see from his letters to Cézanne and Baille during these years of failure and poverty how he tried to atone for his perseverance in his disobedience to her by frequent reference to her devotion and the impossibility of his drawing upon her slender resources any further. But though he eventually relinquished his anarchic bohemianism and turned to competitive ambition – a change which is symbolized by his final desertion of poetry for prose – he did so with a great bitterness towards existence and a conscience about his lost anarchic youth which was to appear, as we shall see, under many guises of self-accusation and attempted apology in his later work. This sense of guilt

about his lost youth was not, I think, completely re-
solved until his personal martyrdom on behalf of society's
outcast, Dreyfus.

His return to Paris in 1860, after his failure in the
examination at Marseilles, meant the final end of his life
with Cézanne and Baille in the countryside round Aix.
His letters to them in the next five or six years are filled
with thwarted schemes to leave the horrors of his Paris
penury and return – a happy release which he realized
only in imagination as the ending of his first novel *La
Confession de Claude*. He was not in fact to return to the
South until the production at Marseilles in 1867 of his
play *Les Mystères de Marseille* in which he collaborated
with his earliest childhood friend Marius Roux. He also
sought refuge in the Midi during the Franco-Prussian
War. But it is, perhaps, significant that, after his career of
success began in real earnest, he only returned there once,
to stay at L'Estaque, near Marseilles, where he wrote
the bitter idyll of *Une Page d'Amour*, a combination of the
old mood and the new; otherwise he is only concerned
with the Aixois as an object of revenge for past insults.

If he could not return to his boyhood, then at least his
boyhood friends could come to him, and this he is also
constantly urging and scheming for in his letters to
Baille and Cézanne. It was as a result of his prodding that
Cézanne defied his prosperous father and came to study
art in Paris. The atmosphere of the art schools was not,
however, sympathetic to him, and this first visit, at any
rate, was a fiasco. Generous as Cézanne was to his poorer
friend, their attempts at common living were a failure.
Both no doubt were suffering nervously from the strain
of lack of recognition and penurious living, but it is
notable that Zola's note of patronage towards his friend
increases from that time onwards.

Much has been written about this friendship and many detrimental conclusions to both men, particularly to Zola, have been drawn from its gradual decline and collapse. It would seem that the critics expect the boyhood friendship of two men who were ultimately to prove men of genius to be more enduring than that of ordinary persons, but exactly the opposite is surely more likely to be the case. That Zola should envy Paul Cézanne* his small competence from his father, when he himself was starving, is not surprising, nor that he should despise† his friend for not using it as he would have done as a springboard to challenge the world, and Cézanne's generosity can unfortunately only have increased these feelings. Whatever Cézanne's apparent failure during later years, the fact that he was able to realize himself as an artist in those very childhood scenes from which Zola had been driven must have been galling to the frequently unhappy and embittered, if successful author. The harshness attributed to Zola in his portrait of Cézanne in *L'Œuvre* is only indefensible if we make the mistake of supposing that Zola's material success could give him personal happiness. Cézanne, on his side, could not forgive Zola for the self-advertisement, vulgarity and bourgeois opulence of his career. He did not see the bitter disillusion on which it was built, nor did he realize that it was only by this painful path of worldly ambition that Zola could realize himself as an artist, and

---

* His attitude is exactly repeated with Valabrègue, a young man of private means, whom he urged to give up poetry and Provence for Paris and the battle for success. Valabrègue's retirement from Paris to Provence was so unacceptable that he was later taken for the model of the would-be artist with no powers in *L'Œuvre*.

† 'Paul peut avoir le génie d'un grand peintre', he wrote, 'il n'aura jamais le génie de le développer.'

that, had he possessed Cézanne's own small means, he would probably have remained in his idyllic boyhood Paradise, a petty provincial imitator of Hugo and La-martine. Their later coolness over the Dreyfus case was, then, only an externalization of a long conflict, and this political difference itself came from their earlier experi-ences – Zola's period of frustration enlisting him forever on the side of the submerged and outcast, Cézanne's retention of his youthful vision upon the side of order and the status quo.

It is not surprising that Zola's letters to his two friends at this period are full of a desperate longing to return to Aix, for after a few months' attempts in 1860 to work as a clerk at the Docks—an experience which gave him nothing but bitterness and despair—he sank into that existence of day-dreaming and renunciation of life which, as has been suggested, must be connected with his illness of two years before. After a short period of living with his mother, he moved on his own from one wretched furnished room on the left Bank to an-other.* We find him at one time in an attic, in which Bernardin de Saint-Pierre had lived, hungry and half frozen, catching sparrows on the roof and roasting them for food. He read Georges Sand, Musset, Shakespeare, Montaigne, and wrote thousands of verses, some of which were later printed in the monograph of his dis-ciple, Paul Alexis. Already his desire to write a large-scale work is to be seen in his planning of an epic on the Creation, but the main theme of his poetry and *contes* was the idyllic, pastoral dream of love he had left behind in Provence, symbolized in the part mistress, part goddess, part boy-girl companion of his imagina-

* She was, however, usually established somewhere nearby.

tion, Ninon, to whom he addressed his first book of stories.

He made one serious attempt to realize this dream-figure in reality, and it is a measure of the degradation of his circumstances, the naïveté of his youth, and the strange arrogance of his character that this episode took the form of an attempt to reclaim a young but worn-out prostitute by admitting her to his idyllic lovemaking. The hideous failure of this experiment is embodied in his first novel *La Confession de Claude*. As he wrote to Baille at the time, 'Aimez la lorette, elle vous méprisera: méprisez-la, elle vous aimera.' The liaison was not assisted by the circumstances of farcical penury which forced Zola to keep beneath the bedclothes whilst his only pair of trousers were in pawn. The whole love affair must have been an episode of squalor and brutal revelation, as cruel to spirit and pride, as it was physic-ally revolting. The deep impression it left appears not only directly in *La Confession de Claude*, but in the strong, visual emphasis on the more animal aspects of physical love in *L'Assommoir*, *Nana*, *Pot-Bouille* and many other novels. It must have gone far to complete his disgust with his 'bohemian' existence and to end the period of sick rejection of life. This neurotic lethargy was only afterwards to reappear at times of stress in his career of abnormal energy and directed power, and he attacked it fiercely in the character of Lazare in *La Joie de Vivre*. The disastrous liaison, which coincided with the bitter winter of 1861–2, was over by February 1862, when he turned his back on this period of failure by securing a position as clerk at Hachette's bookshop through the good offices of an old friend of his father.

In measurement of time it had been a short period, but in its physical suffering and humiliation it must have seemed eternal, and its consequences were of the greatest importance to his future life. It added to his hatred for poverty, and the lives of the poor, but it also increased both his bitterness against a society which tolerated it and his compassion for the submerged. Like Dickens' work in the blacking factory, it symbolized all the horrors of his childhood conflicts. In his determination to escape from it, he roused himself from the idyllic dreams bred by the hot Provençal sun, and returned to the path of salvation by hard work and regular living to which his mother's finger had always pointed.

He remained with Hachette until 1866. The regular salary he received and the routine of work, though often irksome, restored his mental and physical health, and brought back his self-respect. It was to Hachette that he presented his first book of stories, the *Contes à Ninon*. With considerable justification, they refused it, but he found a publisher in Lacroix. This firm published most of his work down to the second book of the Rougon-Macquart series and, as with many famous authors, the somewhat hard bargain he was forced to accept from a firm of doubtful stability would have come near to wrecking his financial position at the start of his career, had it not been for the vision and generosity of the young publisher Charpentier, who rescued him in the crisis over the publication of *La Curée* in 1872. The *Contes à Ninon* are short pastiches, one of which at least – *La Fée amoureuse* – was written when he was seventeen. They cannot be said to be of much literary value, but there is a psychological interest in the recurrent theme of the deaths of youths, of nymphs, and of newly opened flowers—if his idyllic vision of love is to be preserved, the lovers must die and perish in the first flush of passion and so achieve eternity. It is a favourite nineteenth-century theme.

Next came the publication of *La Confession de Claude*, his first full-scale novel, in 1866. It is a crude, highly coloured work, telling of his life with the prostitute; but in its intensity and in the strong visual aspect of some of the scenes it foreshadows his later powers. Although, when it was written, he was already beginning to be deeply interested in Balzac's work, the psychological analysis is possibly more derived from a writer whom he always admired and whose influence is apparent in his first three novels – Stendhal. The whore in her disintegrating blue satin ball dress sitting sullenly by, when Claude is attempting to treat her as an honoured mistress, or gazing with entranced, silent, almost childish pleasure at the louche company dancing at the tarts' ball, to which her lover has managed to take her by selling his last possessions, is a powerfully macabre figure. Perhaps the most important scene is the dream-like early-morning walk of the pair out of Paris into the country after a night's debauch. Here we can already see the substitution of the Seine countryside for Provence as the land of innocence,* a transference of allegiance which encouraged his pioneer appreciation of the work of Manet and Pissarro and which eventually prompted him to settle at Médan on the Seine where much of his most important work was written. The book ends with Claude casting the harlot back into the gutter, and escaping to his friends in Aix, where dwelt the fantasy mistress Ninon, untarnished by any such physical reality. The whole book is notable for its ruthless denial of the romantic view of harlots beloved by earlier writers and, as such, it looks forward to *Nana*.

* To what extent we may judge by his sharing a country cottage at Bennecourt on the Seine with his Provençal friends Baille, Cézanne and Valabrègue. It is described in *L'Œuvre*.

Both the *Contes à Ninon* and the *Confession de Claude* had a certain success. It is interesting to see how anxious Zola is about their reception in Aix society. He had made full use of his connections with critics and writers at Hachette's to secure good notices, but, by now, his position there was becoming a drain on his time, and M. Hachette, noting the falling off in his work, suggested that he should leave. Luckily for Zola, he had just made a connection in the journalistic world which was to do more than compensate for the loss of his regular salary.

To understand the atmosphere in which Zola was scheming for success, a word must here be said about the state of society in these last years of the Second Empire. Napoleon III had created his régime upon many hopes and grievances, but no section of his supporters was more important than those who wished to exploit the financial possibilities of nineteenth-century industrial development to the full. The Empire gave full scope to men of imaginative and speculative ideas who cared little about moral scruples or conventional bourgeois morality. It broke the hard crust of traditional commercialism, well established enterprise and small-scale venture which had settled upon France during the July Monarchy, and let through the get-rich-quick men, the good-timers, the 'fly' men and the 'wide boys'. As the genuine opportunities for bolder industrial and commercial speculation became exhausted, the merry-go-round could only be kept spinning by vaster public works, bigger and more bogus schemes. Haussmann's rebuilding of Paris had attracted scores of adventurers to the capital from every part of France, particularly from the impoverished Midi. It was of this invasion that Daudet wrote in *Le Nabab*; it was this chase for spoils which formed the central social theme of Zola's *Rougon-Macquart* with its adventurers in all fields—Aristide and Eugène Rougon, and Octave Mouret. One stall in this vast circus was the new popular press, and, by good luck, Zola, himself an adventurer in the literary field, found favour by his bold suggestions with Villemessant, the proprietor of *Figaro* and *L'Évènement*, who was always on the lookout for new journalistic stunts. As a result of his friendship with Cézanne and other young Provençal painters, he was already a friend of Pissarro and other Impressionists. Zola had forsaken his former idol Greuze for Courbet and the realists some while before he deserted his romantic idols in literature. He suggested to Villemessant that he should write a series of attacks on the traditional art of the Paris Salon. The violence and impudence of these attacks and his defence of Manet, whose ' Déjeûner sur l'herbe' and other paintings had just been refused by the Salon, won him just the publicity he required. By the time that the cynical Villemessant, thinking that his work had lost its first shock, dismissed him, his position was established.

It is, however, the nature of his appreciation of Impressionism which is crucial for the study of Zola as a literary artist. His views were published in the collected articles *Mon Salon* in 1866 and a monograph *Édouard Manet* in 1867. For him a work of art could not be judged by the old Greek standards of absolute beauty nor by technical competence, but only as a personal expression of the artist and of his age. Manet's work he praised particularly for his clear and personal vision of nature, his penetration of reality – the clarity of light – 'il voit blond' – and the simplicity of construction – 'il voit par masses'. They were lessons that he was never to forget in his own literary work. That his appreciation of the atmospheric realism of the Impressionist school was

largely literary and in some degree romantic is shown
by his later attack upon the Salon of 1896, by now filled
with Impressionist paintings, in *La Nouvelle Campagne*.
He finds the victory of the school he had championed too
complete, and deplores the uniform luminosity of the
many imitators of Monet. We who have suffered from
many decades of inferior Impressionism can sympathize.
His chief admiration in fact was always for Manet and the
early Courbet rather than for Monet and Pissarro, though
he defended all the school against the early attacks.

In 1866 he also published a collection of general essays,
contributions to various Paris or Midi papers, under the
title of *Mes Haines*. They mark his final departure from
romanticism in literature and his new allegiance to
realism. He attacks romanticism in its decadent form
in the catholic writer Barbey D'Aurévilly and in its
more simple form in the works of Erckmann-Chatrian;
his essay on the latter is notable for its praise of Balzac*
whose work was beginning to dominate his literary ideas.
He wrote in high praise of the Goncourts' *Germinie
Lacerteux*, winning their thanks and a lifelong relationship – friendship it could hardly be called – with Edmond
de Goncourt. In view of the devastating effect of the
Utopianism of Fourier on his own work at the end of
his life, it is interesting, also, to notice that he attacks
the influence of the Utopian Proudhon on the later
paintings of Courbet. He was already, then, well known
as a critic and a parvenu literary figure before the publication of his next two novels.

* Already in 1867 he had written: 'Have you read Balzac? What a
man! He crushes the whole country with his weight.' Soon *Rappel*,
a journal run by Hugo's sons, to which Manet gave Zola an introduction, was to reject an article on Balzac for its too strong defence
of realism.

During this period he took another personal step of the very greatest importance to his future life. At a more respectable lodging, to which his improved position allowed him to move, he met Alexandrine Meley. Alexandrine's background, like so many of the important things in Zola's private life, is obscure. It seems clear, however, that the young man's sympathy was called forth by her position as a deserted mistress, and this sympathy soon led to a closer liaison. When her former lover returned, he blessed the new liaison and made a present of his mistress to Émile. The internal evidence of Zola's novels suggests that, whatever the exact circumstances in which his new relationship began, they were such as to create great stress in his emotional centre for most of his life. One of the most powerful and destructive forces in his novels is the figure of the returned lover, the third party in the domestic set-up – indeed he seems to have had some belief that the first lover of any woman always has a powerful hold on her affections,* a view which must have undermined his own sense of security. The triangular situation is treated from many angles, but always as a source of murder, suicide, madness or general decay.

Nevertheless, for the moment all was well. Alexandrine had bourgeois ambitions, she was a forceful, careful, housewifely woman whose deep devotion to Zola gave him just the mental and physical security which the strain of the intense productivity of these years demanded. She provided a comfortable home in which his friends and disciples could gather around him. She was just such a person as his mother could have wished, and indeed Madame François Zola appears to have welcomed

* It is the basis of Gervaise's tragedy in *L'Assommoir,* and, in different forms, vitally important in *La Terre* and *La Bête Humaine.*

the relationship, however irregular, for she soon settled with them. It seems likely that this acceptance by his mother of the liaison which in some way he clearly felt to be grounded in guilt also created a deep conflict in him for, as we shall see, the mother appears often as an additional figure in the triangular set-up, sometimes in a heroic and wronged role, sometimes more equivocally. Certainly, if some unsettled guilt did attach in his mind to his liaison with Alexandrine, the acceptance of it on grounds of worldly prudence by his mother, who stood for counsels of purity, would add to the dark, hostile side of his relation to her. Here he was, however, petted and cared for by two mothers, and in 1870 he regularized his relationship with Alexandrine by a civil marriage. If, as time went on, and Alexandrine remained childless, both women showed a more stormy side to their natures, and Zola himself began to feel the need for more than mothers, the situation was for many years happy enough to give him the stable background his work needed.

During 1866 he made extra money with pot-boiler melodramas, *Le Vœu d'une Morte* and *Les Mystères de Marseille*. He collaborated in a dramatized version of the latter with his old school friend Marius Roux, and it proved to be the first of his many unsuccessful onslaughts on the theatre. In 1868 he published *Thérèse Raquin* and *Madeleine Férat*. Although *Madeleine Férat* was published later, it is a slightly earlier and far less satisfactory work than *Thérèse Raquin*. Both are direct reflections of his new relationship.

Madeleine Férat opens with a scene at an inn in the Seine countryside, ironically enough very like the one to which Claude took his prostitute mistress in the earlier novel. Madeleine, however, is a girl from a higher class.

She had originally been wronged by a young man who rescued her when she was escaping from the lecherous demands of her guardian. Her romantic convent education is expressly blamed for her lack of moral fibre – a favourite theme in Zola's attack upon bourgeois morality. This former liaison is not known to Guillaume, the hero, when he persuades her to sleep with him* at the inn, though she shows a curious familiarity with the shutters of the bedroom windows. The former lover turns out to be Guillaume's greatest friend who has gone abroad and the book is largely taken up with the tragic hopelessness of a union with such a background. The details would seem to have been a mixture of Zola's earlier, less happy experience already described in *La Confession de Claude*, and his relations with Alexandrine. Although the fullest sympathy is given to Madeleine, the picture can hardly have been pleasing to the future Madame Zola.

More horrifying, however, is the turn which is given to the situation in *Thérèse Raquin*, the first of Zola's books which can lay serious claim to real literary merit. The story is of a loveless marriage arranged in childhood by an ambitious and respectable mother. The torpid young wife Thérèse is suddenly woken up to a passionate, adulterous love by an old friend of her husband's, the attractive Laurent. They plan and carry out a brutal murder of the husband. But in their subsequent marriage, they shrink away from one another in horror, whilst the paralysed mother is the witness of their guilty secret, which she cannot indicate except by her eyes. The plot is rich in references to the domestic pattern we have

* It is suggestive of the maternal role that women played in Zola's life that she accedes to his demands out of maternal pity for his feminine terror during a thunderstorm.

already described, and discloses a terrible nightmare in Zola's mind. Technically it is still worked out in the psychological analysis of interior monologue, a weak imitation of Stendhal; Zola has not yet found how to work this crude analysis into a more objective narrative form. But if it is without the breadth and the richness which mark the greatest of the Rougon-Macquart novels, it has a powerful simplicity and symbolism which are akin to Ibsen and which show perhaps why it was the most successful of all Zola's works in stage adaptation. If it disappointed Zola that his idol Taine refused it the praise he had given to earlier work, its general reception was demonstrative, though often abusive, and gave Zola enough financial success to allow him the breathing space necessary to plan the great series of novels which he already had in mind. The financial success was increased, of course, by the fact that both *Madeleine Férat* and *Thérèse Raquin* were first published in serial form – a nineteenth-century practice which Zola usually followed.

novel first

In 1866, Zola moved to Batignolles, and, although he changed to more spacious houses a number of times in the next few years, he never returned to the Left Bank which had been the source of his failure and poverty. His immediate social circle still consisted of his Provençal friends with the addition of some Impressionist painters like Pissarro and Degas, but he was already on visiting terms with the Goncourts, and in correspondence with Flaubert. By 1869 Paul Alexis, one of his own future literary disciples, had appeared on the scene. He also knew the older school of realist novelists, Champfleury and Duranty. His former circle of painters and Provençals in Paris – the fortuitous result of his Aixois origin – was gradually giving way to a literary group more compatible with his career. When the Franco-Prussian war broke out in 1870 he had already completed the first two novels of the Rougon-Macquart series, which will be treated in the next chapter. *La Fortune des Rougon* was, in fact, being serialized and had to be discontinued.

For Zola then, the war could only be a horrible interruption in his great project. He was excused from military service, since both his mother and wife depended on him. A doctor advised that Alexandrine's health demanded her retirement from Paris, and Zola accompanied them both to Marseilles. He intended to return to Paris, but the rapid march of events cut off the capital from Southern France. When *La Débâcle* was published in 1892, the infuriated military classes accused Zola of cowardice during this period, but their charges seem to have been quite unjustified.

At first, he attempted with Marius Roux to found a new periodical in Marseilles. It is a measure of his abstraction from events that he was surprised to find the moment unripe for such an enterprise. Almost penniless, he journeyed to Bordeaux where Gambetta was forming a government, and here, after some difficulties, he found a livelihood as secretary to a minor minister. On his return to Paris, he walked about the city taking notes, and was arrested at different times by both Government and Communard forces as a spy. Left wing critics have attacked his lack of feeling for the Commune and it is possible that if he had not been isolated from the capital during the war, his political sympathies might have been defined earlier; but it seems probable that, coming at the very outset of his cherished enterprise, both war and revolution could only have appeared as hateful interruptions to his work, and sources of danger to his cherished manuscripts.

Chapter II

LES ROUGON-MACQUART:
PRINCIPAL THEMES

Zola in decline – his disciples – a revival due – Inception of the Rougon-Macquart series – Reasons for new approach – Zola's artistic taste and scientific learning – his Achilles' heel – irrelevancy of the usual criticisms levelled against his vulgarity and insufficient education – The theoretical materialist background of the Rougon-Macquart – Letourneau and Prosper Lucas – Importance of Claude Bernard and *Le Roman Expérimental* in this respect – Influence of Balzac – Henry James' tribute – The Notebooks – Class basis of the Rougon-Macquart – Secondary importance of the general scheme beside the individual novels – Discrepancies in the whole – Zola's general view of society – His politics – Money – Marxism – Sex the central core of his view of social evil – Sexual patterns in his work – Adult promiscuity – immature sensuality the Idyll – Sex and the Garden of Eden – Zola and 'Pornography' – Sex and Death – Before and after Jeanne Rozerat.

THERE has, in the last twenty years, been a rehabilitation or, at any rate, a serious defence of most of the nineteenth-century novelists, whose pretensions – in their own day – were to the highest rank. Zola, however, has continued to lie neglected in the dusty cupboard* to which he had already been assigned

* The decline into which the nineteenth century fell at one period may be well illustrated by the critic H. L. Mencken's remarks in

by many younger French writers in his own lifetime. His work has had considerable direct influence, but this very influence has militated against the survival of his reputation, since it was, in general, exercised upon writers who were always estimable yet always of the second rank. To be largely responsible for George Moore and Arnold Bennett in England, Frank Norris and Dreiser in America, Heinrich Mann in Germany, Jules Romains in France, is an equivocal honour. His reputation would have been happier without the well-meant partisanship of minor followers, happier without a school from which as usual the more remarkable disciples seceded, more particularly, happier without the complicated and fourth-rate cultural superstructure of Naturalism which his fear of the personal foundations of his work and his deep intellectual sense of inferiority caused him to erect. Without followers, without the embarrassingly naïve theories of *Le Roman Expérimental*, he might have been judged as an individual, as one of the great cumbrous, magnificent pithecanthropi of nineteenth-century literature. Viewed in such a light Zola can be seen as the close companion of Balzac, Dickens, and Dostoevsky, a little less than them, for certain defects which I shall try to analyse, but offering, nevertheless, a wonderful, enveloping world as they do, and having, in certain respects, both social and personal, a strange clarity of direct vision which their great fusions of the dream kingdom and the waking world obliterated. It is probable that the deserved re-estimation of his work may not be far distant. It must be remembered that he

A Book of Prefaces, 1917. 'Wells, Bennett, Benson, Walpole, Beresford, Galsworthy, Hichens, De Morgan, Miss Sinclair, Hewlett . . . even the least of them is, at all events, a more complete artist than, say, Dickens, or Bulwer Lytton, or Sienkiewicz, or Zola.'

was nearly thirty years younger than Dickens, the
deeper patterns of whose work – both social and personal – have only begun to be recognized in the last
decade, and that he was identified in his lifetime with
literary and social battles the last rumblings of whose
cannons are still faintly audible today. The full battery
of the shocked and prurient combined was turned upon
Zola's work because if he spoke crudely, he also spoke
morally. As usual, one of the most successful weapons
of the prude and the libertine – and they are always
found in alliance in the face of social honesty – has been
the old philistine club – surely once Goliath's – of self-
satisfied laughter. Zola has been declared not only
obscene, but childishly so, and worse still, old-fashioned
in his obscenity. To read his work seriously has been like
facing the imputation of telling an old dirty joke. It is
a charge which few have cared to incur. If we add to
this the fact that the Rougon-Macquart has the misfor-
tune to appear as a long family chronicle, although it is
in fact a series of separate novels covered by the slender-
est links, we can understand the oblivion to which it
has been assigned. If the present small work does no more
than encourage a few readers to unlock the rusty cupboard which contains so much delight it will have served
its purpose.

It is interesting to speculate at what date Zola began
to imagine the vast scheme which was to occupy some
twenty-five or more years of his life. We know that, even
in his early poetic projects, he always inclined towards
the epic; but the Creation and the Fall* are not unusual
subjects upon which young poets centre vague ambitions

* We shall see, however, that for personal, psychological reasons
the Fall and Paradise inevitably played some part even in the final
realistic work.

with ideas as vague concerning their realization. Such inchoate hopes can hardly be regarded seriously as pointers to what Zola was actually to achieve. It may well be that, though *Thérèse Raquin* had shown him his powers of creation and formal organization, both it and *Madeleine Férat* had proved that the violent conflicts within him could not be happily satisfied by transference to paper on a purely personal level. It is notable that the psychological approach, the result of his admiration for Stendhal and the most immediate avenue of escape from his overturned Romantic idols, was thereafter only to be resumed partially in the deep despair of *La Joie de Vivre* of 1884, but not entirely until 1890. Determination to put the years of failure behind him was now his overruling passion.

Nothing perhaps can have seemed so serious a bar to achievement as his comparative lack of education. Education and taste were the two things he lacked to place him on a level with the classes he envied and despised. It is an ironic fact that it was ultimately to be in exactly these two spheres that the society he conquered was to be revenged upon him. Energy and riches can give a man control over these two citadels of the governing classes at a comparatively late stage in life, but if they are to be well founded, if good taste and learning are to be worn with the ease and confidence which are indispensable in the eyes of those to whom they are second nature, they can only be acquired by an adult person if he is endowed with humility as well as imitative powers. Humility was the least of Zola's qualities, though he had more than enough of the related but less helpful characteristic of lack of self-confidence beneath his enormous will to power. It is not therefore surprising that the somewhat correspondence-course nature of his

self-acquired education, with its cocksure dogmatism and
patent-leather up-to-dateness, should have been a target
for his critics both in his lifetime and after; while the
nouveau riche vulgarity of taste exemplified so well in
the over-lavish, expensive junk-shop furnishing of his
villa at Médan, which advertised the huge financial
success of his work, was a perpetual source of amusement and ridicule to his detractors. In an age when
intellectual materialist dogmatism was giving place to
modish 'croyances' and a sceptical approach to science,
Zola clung to his hard-won materialist knowledge with a
provincial assumption of modernity, partly it is true
from a crudity of intellect, but partly also from a deep
and thoughtful distrust of the ultimate social implications
of the new spirit of faith. In an age, too, when ostentatious splendour was being rejected as vulgar by those
who favoured an etiolated elegance of taste perhaps no
less vulgar, Zola still clung to an eclectic display of
riches that surpassed the Second Empire at its own game.
It is easy to say that such determinations do more credit
to his heart than to his head or eye, but the socialism
which he built upon his crude materialism was a more
meaningful reaction to the contemporary social structure than fin-de-siècle despair; while against the de-
corative horrors of Médan must be set the great understanding of Impressionism which is implicit in his own
work and the strength which his very vulgarity gave to
his writing.

The mistake, in fact, which most critics have made is
to extend the ridicule which they express for his superficial materialist philosophy and the vulgarity of his home
from his life to his works. Vulgarity and excess do exist
in his novels, a surface lack of subtlety, at times an irksome over-sureness, but these less happy features are

integrally woven into a pattern of great complexity, modified by a descriptive power that proceeds from a very subtle sense of atmosphere, and invested with a dramatic force which springs from personal despairs and doubts as deep and complex as those of the greatest of the nineteenth-century novelists.

There is, however, a certain logic in the fate which made the hard-won fortresses of education and taste the weak defence-posts against which 'informed critics' have directed their successful attacks upon his work – how successful may be seen from the smiles which greet his name at most literary functions even today. For it was Médan, with its profusion of Japanese prints, Greco-Roman statues, ormolu clocks, Sèvres vases and medieval missals, which was the culminating expression of his material victory. With his vulgar taste he cocked a snook at the forces he had conquered, though in his naïveté he thought he was making a salon entry. It was under the cover of the scientific arguments from the works of Dr. Prosper Lucas on heredity and atavism and from Letourneau's *Physiology of the Passions* – a whole mischmasch of somewhat outdated materialist psychology and retailed Darwinism* – that he found courage to launch the work which was to be the artistic crown of his existence. It is easy to understand that, after the humiliations of his early manhood, he should feel the need of 'serious' and respectable intellectual parentage for the birth of his child, especially when one knows how deeply suppressed were the personal motivations of his work, and that he must have realized what hostility and outcry the violence of his social attacks would inevitably unleash. We may be thankful to M. Letourneau

* Darwin, however, was translated into French in 1862, and published with a preface by Bernard in 1866.

and Dr. Lucas for providing the justification which his feelings of inferiority required, but we need not take very seriously the array of medico-psychological jargon with which the notebooks for the early Rougon-Macquart novels are filled, for as we shall see the hereditary aspect of the novels was never allowed to get in the way of Zola's creative genius. Indeed, this somewhat pathetic aspect of the inception of his great work might well have been forgotten, had not his disciple Céard later introduced him to the works of the materialist psychologist Claude Bernard, and so led him to publish in 1880, at the most controversial moment of his career, following the publication of *L'Assommoir* and *Nana*, a theoretical defence of his work – *Le Roman Expérimental*, in which he attempted to transfer the scientific views of Bernard to the sphere of literature. Few of the theoretical manifestos of great artists have been adequate to their works but it has to be said that *Le Roman Expérimental* is peculiarly silly. It is not surprising that, drawing attention as it must have done to the démodé scientific and philosophical theories which were the jumping-off point of the Rougon-Macquart novels, it should have done immeasurable harm to Zola's claims to be regarded as a serious artist.

However impoverished and outdated the scientific material on which Zola worked so hard in the Bibliothèque Nationale during the years immediately before the Franco-Prussian War, it did provide a framework, cavalierly though it was later to be treated, within which his overflowing emotions and creative powers could be confined. Without the careful genealogical tables of the Rougon-Macquart family with their pompous notes of inherited characteristics, regressions to maternal grandmothers on the intellectual side and dormant physical paralysis derived from the paternal great-uncle, without the atavism and the heredity, there could have been no Rougon-Macquart family. Without the Rougon-Macquart family, with its three branches each stretching into a different social sphere, the total picture of Second Empire society could not have been presented. So rigid an initial arrangement might have petrified in the hands of a lesser artist, but for Zola, often unconsciously, 'the history of a family under the Second Empire' was an organic creation, amidst whose changes and growths both the family of the Rougon-Macquart and the Second Empire itself were often to be pushed from the scene. This organic nature of the great work, I shall hope to show, derived from the fact that under all the scientific ideas of heredity, even beneath the fierce attack on society, the novels had their roots in deep personal aspects of the author's life – aspects which could find their answer in social analysis, because his own inner conflicts were directly related to the social conflicts of the time.

There was, however, one immediate and powerful influence, far greater and more penetrating, that directed the form which his work was to take. We have seen that one of the great discoveries during his impoverished life on the Left Bank had been the works of Balzac, and his admiration for the *Comédie Humaine* grew steadily, outweighing that of Stendhal, forming a ground of dissension with Flaubert during the early days of their friendship. A caricature by André Gill, made when Zola became famous, shows the bust of Balzac returning the later novelist's salute, and Zola was both proud and pleased with the tribute. Comparisons between the *Comédie Humaine* and the *Rougon-Macquart* are not very fruitful; the whole social outlook of the two writers is so completely different, their views of the mainsprings of human conduct so remote from one another, their conceptions of the purpose of existence so alien. But there remains in each, for all the differences of their thought, a striking likeness in their passionate interest in power and energy – qualities which they both possessed in abnormal degree – and this gives to their work a common quality of force and violence, of giant proportion, always under control, yet always, it would seem, on the point of breaking loose from its creator. In any case, Zola's admiration for Balzac was probably decisive in determining the vast scope of the Rougon-Macquart series.

It is impossible not to be impressed by the conviction of ultimate achievement with which Zola presented his original scheme for the ten novels, eventually to increase and grow into twenty, to his publisher Lacroix in 1868. Henry James' tribute is an apt expression of awe: 'No finer act of courage and confidence is recorded in the history of letters. The critic . . . returns again and again to the great wonder of it, in which something so strange is mixed with something so august. Entertained and carried out almost from the threshold of manhood, the high project announces beforehand its inevitable weakness and yet speaks in the same voice for its admirable, its almost unimaginable strength.'*

In the ninety volumes of manuscript notes for the Rougon-Macquart deposited by Madame Zola in the Bibliothèque Nationale we have an unique opportunity of seeing a great literary work in formation. Only fragments of these notes have been printed, partly by Zola's

---

* Barbusse's tribute is less elegant but more exact: 'There is hardly an example in the history of intellectual creations of a man seeing in advance with so much precision the concrete contours of a multiform work.'

son-in-law Maurice Le Blond in his prefaces to the standard editions, partly by M. Henri Massis in his *Comment
Zola composait ses romans*, itself a remarkable work
written when its author was only a youth. What does
emerge, apart from the immensely painstaking docu-
mentation and the brilliant formal planning of the novels,
are the many changes which inevitably took place over
the years, though the original grandeur of conception
was increased rather than diminished. These became
more than ever necessary after the fall of the Empire
in 1870. History contributed the final dramatic ending
to Zola's epic, but the epic had, of course, to be re-
planned. As a result many events were telescoped and
this accounts for the overcrowded canvas of many of the
novels.* Even before the composition of the introductory
novel *La Fortune des Rougon* we find many changes of
name for both the Rougon and the Macquart branches
of the family, and the Mouret branch does not appear in
the first notes.

The emergence of these three rivers is important, for
with them the broad class structure of the analysis of
Second Empire society is determined. From the legiti-
mate Rougon heirs of the crazy source of the family,
Tante Dide, sprang the hard, ambitious, intellectually
brilliant set of adventurers who descend like hungry dogs
upon the bleeding quarry of rich Imperial Paris, tearing
it to pieces, until in its final death throes they emerge
themselves exhausted, effete and vicious as the original
aristocracy that they have despoiled. Zola's habitual
ambivalence in relation to society is illustrated very
clearly in the novels which deal with this ruling-class

* *La Débâcle*, for example, the novel of the Franco-Prussian War,
was originally planned to deal with the Franco-Italian campaign of
1859.

branch of the family. Pierre and Félicité Rougon, the
parents who achieve local power in Plassans, the original
Provençal home town of the family, by backing the
Bonapartist horse in 1851, come in for his most fierce
exposure as representatives of the local Aix-en-Provence
families who had ignored the Zolas in their time of
poverty. Eugène Rougon, their son, however, who rises
to be a principal minister of Napoleon III, is the very
representative of the powerful, ruthless man that
Zola with his ambition and strength of purpose might
have been in the sphere of action,* and it is most notable
that Eugène's success is attained through a hard-won
battle for sexual supremacy, which is made to give him
an almost magical access of force.

The Mourets, in whom are depicted the bourgeoisie,
though illegitimate, are significantly a female line, for
Zola's chief hatred of the bourgeoisie was directed
against its 'mollesse' and 'souplesse'. From the marriage
of Ursule Macquart to a Marseilles tradesman spring the
small bourgeois of Plassans, and from them, in turn,
comes Octave Mouret, like his cousin Eugène an adventurer, who with quick Midi wits and ruthless use of his
sexual charms, preys upon the small tradesmen of Paris,
and founds the first great monopoly store 'Au Bonheur
des Dames' upon the ruin of the very class from which
he is sprung. Once again Zola's attitude is somewhat
ambiguous. For the central core of the bourgeoisie he
has nothing but hatred; mean or spendthrift, pious or
adulterous, they either fade out of life in a devitalized
miasma of prudery, are swallowed up in the fatty richness

* Paul Alexis, Zola's chief disciple, took this view. But Zola's
son-in-law Le Blond disagreed and thought the character founded on
the minister Rouher. Zola in his notes calls Eugène 'un Mornay au
petit pied'.

of a complacent gluttony, or are torn to pieces in a hysterical effort to break free from their domestic prison. But for Octave Mouret, who dares to tread upon his own kind, his admiration is direct. He even attempts, in the unsatisfactory Christian Socialist ending of *Au Bonheur des Dames*, to resolve the contradiction between his belief in the survival of the fittest with his hatred of cut-throat morality.

From the main illegitimate branch of the Macquart come the proletariat, the submerged section of this fierce competitive society – vicious, ignorant, pathetic in their small but hopeless ambition only to survive – they are yet shown as the most productive of ultimate diversity because of the very formlessness which marks them as a class. Gervaise, for example, the tragic heroine of *L'Assommoir* and the type of the slum-dweller, is the mother of Étienne, the growing revolutionary, Claude, the artist, Nana, the high-class tart, and Jacques, the criminal. Though Zola's lack of illusion about the poor made him an object of radical attack in his own day, and of censure from Communist writers like Barbusse in ours, his loathing for their degradation is accompanied by a certain pity. For the independent workers, and their numbers were not large at that time, he has an admiration as great as that for successful men, and less uneasy. No nineteenth-century novelist, perhaps, succeeded so well in depicting the courage and honesty of the individual, aspiring workman of the century, and he does so with a lack of sentimentalism and a real understanding of the necessary limitations of such a life that is quite unique.

Such an exact class analysis if it had been rigidly adhered to, might well have produced novels that were text-books of political economy or social sermons rather than works of art. Zola, however, was too great an artist and too determinedly objective a writer to fall into this error more than occasionally. In the first place, though one may speak of his 'pity', his 'admiration', his 'hatred', these are seldom stated explicitly. Zola gave up a psychological approach to character after *Thérèse Raquin* until the deliberate reversion of *La Bête Humaine* – one of the few examples of his scheme controlling him, rather than he the scheme, for it had been planned from the start, and in order to write it he had to introduce a completely new figure as late as 1890. Nor are his occasional personal homilies very important. Such moral judgments as appear are implicit in the descriptive narrative and the speech of the characters. But more important than this artistic objectivity, to which he adhered so earnestly, is his disregard of the total formal structure of the series if an individual novel seemed to demand it. Important divergences exist even in the basic class construction of the Rougon-Macquart. The supreme example of the bourgeoise, the handsome, sleek, treacherous Lisa Quenu, the central character of *Le Ventre de Paris*, is the eldest of the proletarian Macquart line. Angélique, the idealized symbol of true love in *Le Rêve*, is the daughter of the political informer and procuress, Sidonie Rougon. The important fact is that, though Zola needed the formal scheme of the series to liberate his vast energies, and though he was often unaware himself of its secondary nature, most of the novels of the series, and, certainly, the best, were carefully planned as separate units, and if they interfered with the whole, the whole had to be remoulded. Frequently the members of the Rougon-Macquart are only formally the central characters, the real emphasis of the novels being placed upon other social groups, of whom the adventurers and outcasts from Plassans form useful observers.

Étienne Lantier, the son of Gervaise Macquart, for example, who finds employment in a mining town, is able to observe his new surroundings with an exactitude which would be absurd in a local inhabitant, and so it is with Jean Macquart, freshly arrived among the peasants of *La Terre*, or Nana, as she rises to the heights of the demi-monde. Such Rougons and Macquarts are useful eyes – Zola's eyes. He made little attempt, beyond an occasional explanatory reference which almost always appears forced, to connect the members of the family in one book with those in another. Such characters as do reappear have little consistency, except for Nana whose future had probably already been planned in detail when she appeared as the vicious little girl of *L'Assommoir*. Jacques Lantier, the central character of *La Bête Humaine*, was simply invented after the novels, in which his branch of the family appeared, had been published, and what evidence they give of the general family background clearly precludes his existence. It was not the family heredity, nor even the theoretical class analysis that the family provided, with which Zola was concerned, however he may have wished to think so, but particular patterns of life which made immediate appeal to him. Nevertheless by establishing a broad general scheme and fulfilling it equally broadly, he insured that his artistic powers should be exercised over the widest possible field.

Zola's view of society as a whole was conditioned by the dichotomy which was the subject of the first chapter. His sense of personal social humiliation in childhood and adolescence gave him a hatred for all sections of society, though for the poorest he retained an emotional compassion as great as his physical disgust. This general pessimism inclined him to a despairing, almost anarchic view of society. On the other hand, his natural ambition, energy and personal success in the material sphere could not allow him to remain content with such pessimism. On this side of his nature, he was more suited to be an optimistic radical, and indeed his reverence for the scientific advance of the century made him a staunch adherent of Progress. His reading of materialist philosophy, however, led him into the realm of scientific determinism and this, in general, supported the generally pessimistic side of his nature – so that his eventual picture of society in the Rougon-Macquart was of an organism so complex, that unless like the nihilists one was prepared to destroy it all in one holocaust, there was no alternative but to wait for the effects of education and scientific invention to take their appointed course.

Zola's approach to knowledge was analytical, as the notebooks show. His method of work was to collect as much information as possible and then to extract an analysed scheme. The final result of his selection often appears as too great a simplification of the material he was studying, but, nevertheless, the effects of the complexity of the subject he studied in such detail are implicit in his books: his awareness of the great multiplicity of interdependent strands that lay beneath the apparent simplicity only served to emphasize his deterministic attitude towards society and added to the natural disinclination of his compassionate heart to judge the behaviour of individuals. The objective analysis which he gives of the corrupt, putrescent society of the Second Empire is filled with burning indignation, but only rarely does this find relief in attacks upon particular characters. For many years, almost throughout the publication of the Rougon-Macquart novels, he defended this objectivity on the aesthetic grounds of the Naturalist creed, though his personal identification with the misery which he described was always pushing him towards some more positive attitude. There is a very close affinity between his view of contemporary French society and that of Karl Marx – the same brilliant simplification, the same puritanical horror, the same disgust at human waste, not only among the poor, but in all classes. For Zola, however, no manifesto call to arms was possible, he felt too keenly the individual lives he described, their circumscribed wills, their despairing unhappiness, their intense if short-lived pleasures, to be confident of the cleansing power of action. Only in *Germinal* (1885) did he evidence any faith in the possibility of mass action as the necessary solution. From that time, it is true, his novels showed society more and more in its group aspects and less in individuals, but he did not again suggest any sympathy for the idea of socialism brought about by the masses themselves.* He was not by nature a man who could easily accept the idea of violence, against which the whole of his luxury-loving, bourgeois taste and the great gentleness of his character revolted. However violent his own inner emotions, physical and external violence, which is a constant feature of his novels, always appears as a symbol of the self-destructive, corrupt elements in life.

In this mistrust of mass action, he resembles Dickens, whose early life and education led him to a similar view of society, veering from a vague political radicalism to a sort of pessimistic anarchism. But, whereas Dickens' pessimism increased as a result of the progressive deterioration of his domestic life, Zola's was eventually dissolved by his fruitful liaison with Jeanne Rozerat;

* In *L'Argent*, however, one of the more sympathetic characters is shown as actuated by Marx's writings.

in both cases, however, the pessimism of their works
was in direct contrast with the external success and
bonhomie of their lives. Not a little of the violence of
their novels originates from this split in their personalities.

Zola, like Dickens, mistrusted all the political parties.
But whereas Dickens' political scepticism came from
his view that all power was a corrupting influence on the
will, Zola's contempt came largely from a general dis-
belief in the strength of the human will either for good
or for evil. With his own abnormally developed will and
energy, Zola was, perhaps, over-inclined to regard
humanity as shifting, windswept sand whose apparent
stability or direction was liable at any minute to be
changed by some chance desire or momentary difficulty.
For the ruling classes and bourgeoisie there were the
varying shades of Legitimist, Orléanist, Ultramontane,
Bonapartist or Republican which were worn either for
some immediate gain, from prejudice or from social
snobbery. Ministers, deputies, judges and bureaucrats
alike are twitched on the ends of the golden wires of the
great money adventurers who had made the Empire, and
who, like Aristide Rougon, rushed to and fro to patch
the breaks in the rotting nets of their vast, speculative
fishing for gold. The events of 1848 and 1851 had certainly
lent colour to the view that, for large numbers of men
and women, political ideals were coats to be worn according to the weather. Zola believed that the components
of the social organism were decaying and would in their
time die, as the whole edifice of the Second Empire
crumbled in the course of the Rougon-Macquart, or as
the small shops decayed and eventually fell prey to the
monopolist competition of 'Au Bonheur des Dames'.
Occasionally the pressure of hunger upon the workers

might cause a sudden revolt in the course of which the unadaptable bourgeois might suffer. Étienne, the defeated strike leader of *Germinal*, hears the picks of the miners beneath the ground as he leaves the village and reflects that they sound like an ever-growing army stretching into the future. This ending suggests that Zola did consider the possibility of the decay being arrested by mass class action. But it is a momentary mood. In the main, he regarded revolutionaries as dreamers like Souvarov, the Russian anarchist of *Germinal*, or Florent, the duped hero of *Le Ventre de Paris*, or as a particular variation of the prevailing selfish knave who had assumed such opinions because too many were already sharing the pickings of the orthodox parties. The opinions of 1848 he particularly despised. The plotters who gather round Florent are sincere, but their group is riddled with police spies, and their whole conspiracy is treated as a farce. As a rule, however, '48 men are merely workers who are too lazy and cunning to work for independence – tramps like Jésus Christ in *La Terre*, rogues like old Antoine Macquart, or 'flâneurs' and 'maquereaux' like Lantier, the lover of Gervaise. Pity is reserved only for the youth Silvère Mouret and his girl companion who, in the Plassans rising of 1851, fell as duped sacrifices to the roguery of those who had encouraged their enthusiasm. But the love of Silvère and his vivandière has a special symbolic significance for Zola as we shall see in the analysis of the sexual motives of the Rougon-Macquart novels. Equally futile are most purely individual revolts against social convention, for they are usually made without consideration of their consequences and the human will is not strong enough to endure. Hélène Mouret with her married lover in the garden of *Une Page d'Amour*, Serge Mouret, the priest with the half-wild girl Albine in the garden of Paradou, Renée with her stepson in the tropical gardens of *La Curée* are doomed to failure. The knot, social or personal, is too hard for the individual to untie.

Nevertheless, for Zola, as for Dickens, the picture of society which his analysis produced was too horrible to be passed over without some attempted solution. When the radical newspapers objected to his picture of the working classes in *L'Assommoir*, Zola declared that as an artist he was concerned only with truth, not with opinions. This aesthetic creed of the naturalists was his constant sermon; but, nevertheless, it is possible to see a series of attempted solutions in the Rougon-Macquart novels which taken in conjunction with changes in his private life bridge the apparent gap between the objective novels of the family chronicle and the 'romans à thèse' and the propaganda novels of 1894 onwards. The first faint positive note is struck in *Son Excellence Eugène Rougon*, published in 1876. This eldest son of the eldest branch gambles for success by helping Louis Napoléon to power in 1851, and, as a reward, becomes a chief minister. At the opening of the book, however, he has fallen from power through court intrigues. But not only is Eugène ruthless in his control of others of weaker will, he is also resolute and patient in the control of his own will, and, by waiting and using events, he returns to power. An important element in his success is his mastery of his lust for the adventuress Clorinde, and his refusal to use sex except as part of the general scheme of his life. Eugène is the first character for whom Zola expresses a certain social approval – not the fool who attempts to alter events, but the man who directs his own advantage in 'the direction in which society is moving'. Such Zola seems to suggest may be the only kind of enlightened behaviour in a deterministic, complex world. It is interesting to contrast this attitude with that of Dickens, for whom ruthless people are almost always villains. Since both writers were ambitious, successful men, the contrast is a curious one. The explanation, I believe, lies in the fact that Zola was able to face the ruthless element in his own campaign for success, because he was a naturally kindly man, whilst Dickens could not do so without acknowledging the deep sadistic element in his emotions.

Eugène Rougon's ride on the crest of the social wave is later repeated in the career of Octave Mouret, who, after using his charm and good looks to conquer the depraved bourgeois world of *Pot-Bouille*, turns the shop 'Au Bonheur des Dames', left to him by his first wife, into the first great Parisian multiple store. But here a different element enters in the person of the heroine Denise, a sort of Pamela, a sweet young shop-assistant whose battle for her virtue eventually wins for her a marriage with her boss. Her charitable impulses and knowledge of the sufferings of shop-assistants make her demand from Octave a co-operative Fourierist organization of the store as the price of her hand. This is a solution more akin to those which Dickens attempted and never found satisfactory. Though there is nothing objectionable in the ending, the mixture of the calculating virginity of Denise and the calculating promiscuity of Octave make it one of the least pleasant of Zola's books.

Something of this he must have felt himself, for *La Joie de Vivre* (1884), the next novel, presents charity in a very different light. Pauline, one of the most attractive of Zola's heroines, is possibly a tribute to his wife, who was famous for her good works and to whom he had been

particularly closely drawn during their common har-
rowing experiences at the time of his mother's death in
1880, an episode which also appears in the book. But
however fine the character of Pauline, the futility of the
medical and educational help she organizes for the
ignorant, brutal poor of the seaside village in which she
lives, is clearly a culminating irony in a book of such
pessimism and despair that its title is one of the most
bitter ever bestowed.

We have already seen that, for a moment, in *Germinal*,
published in the following year, Zola came down in
support of workers' action, and there can be little doubt
that the countless tributes from working men did much
to fix his steps in the path of Socialism, though it was not
ultimately to be of the strike-action type portrayed in
the book.

It is not, indeed, until the last two novels of the
Rougon-Macquart that a note of genuine hope for society
is struck. In *La Débâcle*, Jean Macquart, the simple
peasant, with an emotional understanding greater than
his powers of expression, ready and sure in emergency,
is contrasted with the doubt-ridden, impulsive intellectual Maurice. Zola comes down against the revolutionary
ideas of the Communards and in favour of a peaceful,
constructive future in the hands of the working community. In *Le Docteur Pascal* religious superstition and
bourgeois pride destroy the great scientific work of the
hero, but an heir is born, the work has not been wasted,
hope lies in the future. These somewhat naïve conclusions,
expressed even more directly in the trilogy of the three
cities, look directly forward to the busy, hivelike, loving,
co-operative, fecund Fourierist communities of the
novels of Zola's last years. To explain this change by his
association with Jeanne Rozerat and the birth of his two

children would seem too simple. Nevertheless, for Zola, society and sex were closely connected concepts, sexual sterility, social corruption and death, which he so feared, intricately entwined.

To understand fully, then, the change in the social patterns of his work, we must now examine the sexual patterns in the Rougon-Macquart novels and their relation to his own life. For Zola, sex is the Achilles' heel of humanity, responsible parenthood its crowning glory. Sex was a temptation into which a man might be led without the full use of his will, habitual promiscuity was the negation of the will. The sexually promiscuous, in his books, are the indolent, the slipshod, the weak. The sexual act was a loss of energy, a further emphasis of the random futility of humanity in a determined, cruel world. Work – regular hours of writing, regular numbers of words written – was Zola's recipe for success and self-respect. Promiscuity was a sin against work.

Adultery was the besetting sin of the upper classes and the grande bourgeoisie. Zola opposed most strongly the whole system of arranged marriages, their lovelessness, their calculation, their loneliness. *Pot-Bouille* is the story of a community of outwardly respectable bourgeois whose inner life is a continual interchange of partners for the bed, where the husbands frequent high-class prostitutes, and the wives await the sound of the front door closing behind their husbands to open the back door to their waiting lovers, where the servants mimic and mock their masters' infidelities in crude and filthy language that matches the 'ordures' which they throw out in the mornings. Octave Mouret, alone, can be forgiven, for he calculatingly uses sex for his advancement. Entertaining, powerful though it is, the whole book is a little like a 'witty French farce' scrawled on a lavatory wall. The protests of the bourgeoisie, those who had thought *L'Assommoir* so impressive a book, were shrill. But Zola persisted that his picture was just.* From very early in his career he had attacked the emptiness and sentimental emotionalism of the Catholic girls' school, to which even non-practising bourgeois sent their daughters. A rapid, romantic education and an arranged marriage led, he suspected, straight to the adultery of the bored young wife.

The atmosphere of adultery and wasteful promiscuity reigns also in Zola's upper-class novels – differing only from the bourgeois world by its modish frankness, its bored explorations into sexual bypaths, its greater recognition of the cicisbeo. Only in certain devout, Legitimist households is moral laxity frowned upon, and these dark, chilling salons, where the old marquises and generals scorn Imperial vulgarity and Orléanist treachery, seem to wear chastity only as another dried wreath of immortelles upon the tomb of the political and social death of their inhabitants. For the new moneyed barons, the bankers, the financiers, the very centre of the great 'pourriture' of Second Empire society, sex has its particular and deadly peril. Muffat, the Catholic puritan minister, the Baron Deneuilly, whose vast enterprises control all Paris in the book of that name, all the great money lords become the prey of some guttersnipe actress-prostitute who drains the money-blood from them. The naked, middle-aged Muffat, beaten by Nana, as he crawls on all fours like a dog, may come from Otway's *Venice Preserved,* but he is the symbol of all that Zola believed that sexual passion.could do to degrade the

* It must be admitted that Huysmans who helped him with architectural information said that the bourgeois language 'was pitched a tone too low. It is more jesuitical, more shrill'.

powerful will and the adult intellect. Only Eugène Rougon spurning Clorinde, whom he longed to possess, is saved. For the rest, Nana, with her 'belles cuisses', her 'hanches roulantes', her 'gorge superbe', arises from the filth of the slums to be avenged for the degradation of the poor.*

If the energies of the rich were spent and wasted in fruitless, tiring sexual exploits, the poor turned to sex as the only pleasure they could afford – 'le petit plaisir des pauvres'. But they paid for it in further degradation and misery. Ostensibly L'Assommoir, the bistro with its fatal yellow goddess of absinthe, was a sermon against drink, one of the greatest temperance tracts Vizetelly, Zola's English translator, naïvely called it; but it is not really through drink that Coupeau and Gervaise, the good-natured, deserving working-class couple, come to ruin. The false turnings, which Zola clearly marks in the roads that lead Coupeau to the strait-jacket and Gervaise to die in filth and rags, are sexual. It is weakness and desire that make Gervaise forgive Coupeau when he returns drunk to the laundry in mid-afternoon. It is the kiss 'en pleine bouche' that he gives her and her easy acceptance of fuddled lovemaking that spell squalor and ruin. It is Coupeau's 'bon copain' acceptance of his wife's ex-lover as lodger that completes the process. 'Faire dodo' is the fatality of the poor.

Throughout his career Zola was attacked as a pornographic writer – a view which has since been increased in America by large numbers of illicit, hotted-up translations sold by book pedlars and in 'dirty' book shops. Nothing, in fact, could be less attractive than the squalor and disease which surround the sex life of his

---

* Zola's own note for Nana is to the point: 'a gang after a bitch, who is not on heat and who mocks the dogs that follow her.'

poor, the boredom and anxiety that beset his rich in their lovemaking. There are, however, certain romantic love episodes in Zola's work – though they are never cited by the smut salesmen – about which an atmosphere of sensuality and excitement hangs that might be charged with the accusation of pornography. They are all of a very special kind: the innocent love of the very young, a sort of natural lovemaking of Adam and Eve before the fall. This is the declared symbol of *La Faute de l'Abbé Mouret* in which the young priest Serge is nursed back from fever by a wild, natural girl Albine in a ruined garden of an eighteenth-century château. But the avenging angel in the person of the savage, puritanical friar drives them out and the end is death and sterility. For Angélique, the girl-heroine of the 'roman bleu', *Le Rêve*, the first kiss of marriage is followed by death. For Sylvère and his girl companion there is only death from the enemy firing squad. On occasion the more sophisticated, even the depraved, may seek to return to this Paradise in a desperate attempt to get free of the horror of existence, but the end for them is the same. Renée, the young, consumptive society woman, tries to recreate childish happiness in an affaire with her seventeen-year-old depraved stepson Maxime in the tropical gardens of their Paris mansion. Nana's only genuine innocent happiness comes with Zézé, the young boy, in the garden of the country house which Count Muffat has rented for her. Not only are all these idyllic, sensual love affairs sterile and deadly, but their childlike aspect is marked in a peculiar form. They are essentially adolescent, and this in a very pathological way, they have a curious intersexual appearance – Maxime, Zézé, even Serge are pretty youths, and for Nana and Renée excitement comes originally when they are seen decked in women's clothes. Paradise then is not only illusory, it is a very hot-house land.*

The answer to this sexual despair, the very core of his social pessimism, lies in Zola's own life. Nothing in Zola's early days in Paris had helped him to escape from his retrospective view of happiness, and his marriage seems to have proved to be no solution. Alexandrine was a good wife, ambitious, thoughtful for his needs, strong in character, emotionally profound. But she appears to have been only a supplement to his already deep mother-fixation. Had they been able to have children, all this might have been changed, but, unfortunately, this was not to be so. It was a tragedy that weighed upon them as the years passed, until they would lie side by side at night in terror, each knowing what was in the other's mind – the thought of final extinction, of death. *La Joie de Vivre*, conceived during the breakdown which followed his mother's death, recounts this in horrifying terms. Sterility and death, then, mark sexual union for Zola, and the 'natural' childlike mating which appears as an escape turns out to be an etiolated union of Narcissus and Circe amidst the poisonous tendrils of some tropical cactus. Here surely lies the key to the horror and despair of Zola's world, and it is only after his fruitful union with Jeanne Rozerat – a union which caused such misery to poor Alexandrine – that the picture changes. Already in *La Débâcle*, more openly in *Le Docteur Pascal*, and finally in *Paris*, the end of the long trilogy of Abbé Froment's road to a new faith,† a note

* In the latter part of his life, in attacks on Puvis de Chavannes and Burne-Jones, and in *Paris* Zola was particularly violent against their sexless epicene representations of human beauty.

† It is notable that the family life which won the Abbé from despair was that of a high-minded union not blessed by any ceremony religious or civil.

of hope appears – fecundity, work no longer as a drug but in happy knowledge that it will be carried on by posterity, a socialism gradual but sure because there is all the future in which to complete it – this was the faith which Jeanne Rozerat gave to Zola. It saved him from morbidity, and it ended his career as a great writer. The 'black poet' changed to a naïve propagandist, repeating the old characters and themes of the Rougon-Macquart, but with a discursiveness, a lifelessness and a stilted preaching which are the negation of his art.

Chapter III

LES ROUGON-MACQUART:
THE FORM OF EXPRESSION

Artistry and journalism in Zola's work – his assaults upon his readers' emotions – impressionist writing – careful balance of character and incident – 'atmospheric' devices – analysis of his 'black' poetry – too great concern with exact detail – animal symbols – adherence to unities of time and place – cinematic quality of Zola's work – his preoccupation with the human will – no preoccupation with single characters until Rougon-Macquart series was complete.

AFTER the publication of *L'Assommoir*, with its phenomenal, scandalous success, Flaubert, while praising the novels highly, was moved to protest against Zola's increasing use of publicity. To this, Zola was quick to reply that he was not only artist but journalist, and that both personalities must find expression. There is a certain disingenuousness in this answer, of which Zola himself may not have been fully conscious, for it implied that the artist expressed himself in the novels, the journalist in pamphlets and articles. Zola had learnt the value of publicity from his early career as a shock leaderwriter, and he never ceased to use such shock methods to force his work on the public. But it was not only by publicity that the Rougon-Macquart novels were turned into best-sellers and their author into a very rich man. Readers might have been brought to the novels by preparatory newspaper articles, correspondence and prearranged controversy, they would not have been persuaded to stay. Then, as now, the average reader wanted a saccharine, a sugar-cake world; it could only be by bludgeoning and violence that he would be persuaded to assist at a black mass in which his sacred bourgeois creeds were recited backwards, his angels of virtue revealed as seven deadly sins, and the very Host of his self-esteem was spat upon. The strength of the greatest Rougon-Macquart novels lay in exactly this kind of assault and battery; an attack, planned with the greatest care and conscientious artistry by a writer whose devotion to the creed of art for art's sake was by no means lip service, and carried out by a journalist of genius, who frequently failed to see that his literary devices were stale and obvious, but whose force of expression was great enough to prevent the reader from seeing it too. Though artist and journalist were frequently at loggerheads, in the earlier novels, they gradually learnt to work together to form a novelist who was unique.

The optimistic, cocksure bourgeois world of the 'forties and 'fifties was giving way to fin-de-siècle melancholy and ennui; all but the most obtuse felt the rotten boards creak beneath their feet, saw the scaffolding tremble above their heads. Zola, in his luxury and success, was seldom unconscious of these rumblings and groanings, and by his art, his force, his hatred, compassion and vulgarity, he drove the public to pile up his fortune as they queued to peer at the very hell they had spent most of their lives in avoiding. The peepshows were cleverly labelled – the Sanctity of the Family, the Honour of the Army, the Virtues of the Poor, the Ideals of the Artist, the Traditions of the Peasantry,

the Splendour of the Church, the Soundness of Finance
– and in each there lay a putrescent corpse, far more
terrible than the skeleton the poor reader had shut away
so carefully in the cupboard of his own guarded conscience. Even now, the greatest of the novels – *L'Assommoir, La Terre, Germinal* – have the quality of nightmares;
how much more appalling must they have been for the
contemporary reader. And, as from nightmares, there
was no means of escape. Each world of horror was air-
tight, a little cell, like that where Coupeau danced his
delirium tremens, carefully secured and locked, carefully padded but not too much; Zola the artist saw to
that. After the victim had come out, of course, he would
cry triumphantly 'Life isn't like that. Realism, indeed!
Why, no peasant talks like that. Spontaneous combustion, insanity, haemophilia all in one chapter, ridiculous!
Five deaths from drink in one novel, absurd!' But he
would always remember that it was real while it lasted,
and that somewhere inside himself there was a twin
horror which had been exposed. If there were moments
when Zola the artist failed to convince, when the detail
was too careful, when a chink of sunlight crept into the
black room, then before the reader could stir himself,
wake and declare that he knew it hadn't happened, Zola
the journalist was ready with a truncheon, some vast
episode of peculiar force or horror, to bludgeon him
into submission – Françoise making her way past the
endless sea of ripe, golden corn, beneath the baking
sun of *La Terre*, suddenly and brutally assaulted by
Buteau, less brutally, less completely by Jean – the
reader's credulity wavers. The atmosphere, the scene,
the growing lust of the men, Zola the artist has built
these up with complete surety, but two rapes in the
afternoon? No; we can't quite take that. All right, says

the journalist, what about that cry from the centre of the cornfield – Palmyre, the pathetic cripple girl, the beast of burden, has broken beneath her load, a blood-vessel burst in the glare of the sun, and then, in case the reader is still resisting, the tall, gaunt figure of La Grande, the aged peasant woman, advances and prods the body with her stick, 'Dead', she says, 'well, that's better than a wretched burden on others.' The episode is complete; the life of the peasantry, one feels sure, is like that – hard, mercenary, brutal. 'Il faut avoir la passion,' said Zola, 'un souffle, un et fort, qui emporte le lecteur jusqu'à la fin.'

Zola's whole artistic approach made him particularly fitted to carry out this task. He saw each novel as a separate picture, planned the whole shape in advance as would a painter. We have already said that the Rougon-Macquart series as a whole with its science, its heredity, even its social analysis, was always subordinate to the needs of the individual novels, equally the internal considerations of each novel – characters, events, time, place – were all subject to the demands of the logic of the total book.

From the earliest notes made for the series, it is clear that Zola realized his need to ensure this air-tight quality in his novels if they were to succeed. He affirms his decision to avoid Balzac's methods of presenting more than one group of society in any particular book. It is only in the later books like *Paris* that the very poor and the very rich are shown together, and it is clear from the unsuccessfully crude contrast, with its obvious moralising flavour, that his earlier decision was a wise one. His cuts into society were, in general, horizontal and not vertical. Within these horizontal sections, he planned each succeeding chapter as a separate step in the progressive logic of the whole. His own words describe this method very exactly: 'Instead of the flowing analysis of Balzac, establish fourteen or fifteen powerful masses, within this framework analysis may be made step by step, but always from above. Everybody in the world analyses in detail nowadays, I must react against this through the solid reaction of masses, of chapters, through the logic, the thrust of the chapters, succeeding each other like superimposed blocks; by the breath of passion, animating all, flowing from one end to another of the work.' Logical steps fused into a whole by passion, and by another quality which he does not mention, acute atmospheric sensitivity. A solidly established formal scheme given movement by emotional force and life by shimmering atmosphere – an Impressionist painting of the highest order. It is not 'Naturalism' but impressionistic technique which explains Zola's greatness.

The neurotic obsessions of artists are often a clue to their greatest gifts. We have seen that Zola's acute fears of death reflect the inner theme of his great work. In 1881 and 1882, when the serious nervous tension of his life came nearest to a breakdown, a number of symptoms showed themselves. Delusions of clouds of birds relate probably to the importance of animals in his work, which will be discussed later in this chapter, but there was also revealed a strong obsession with numbers, their relationships, and the good auguries of certain primary numbers and their various multiplications. Such numerical and counting obsessions are familiar pathological features of nervous disorders. A supreme example of their control of a writer almost to the point of insanity is to be found in the work of the Marquis de Sade, and the effect upon his work is direct – each sexual exploit is repeated in a series in which progressive numbers of

persons participate until the whole is reduced to a cata-
logue which can only be regarded as a written version of
the repeated touching of objects for luck, one of Freud's
examples of the pathology of everyday life. Zola's
obsession with numbers was only a distortion of the
strong proportional sense which is the underpin of his
whole fictional structure. Each character, each aspect,
each symbol must be given an exactly related stress in
the novel. After reading the preparatory notes for *L'Assommoir*, for example, it becomes apparent that every incident in the book has been prepared and fitted into the
frame like the pieces in a jigsaw puzzle. Inevitably, on
occasion, this 'made' aspect of the book manifests itself
to the reader, for if Zola had great artistic force, he had
less artistic taste. But, if the central symbol of the old
undertaker and his conversations with Gervaise concerning the comfort of the grave for the poor are too
obvious a preparation for the final scenes in which he
removes her mouldering, forgotten corpse, there are
other aspects of the same careful prearrangement which
are so well contrived within the narrative and so swept
along by the force of the novel that it would require a
very detached reader to detect them. Gervaise, for
example, asks no more of life than a small corner in
which to lay her bones in old age, the little country
retreat of the poor slum-dweller, and the reader is so
struck by the pathos of this simple wish, and the actual
horror of her decline, that he is unlikely to notice the
heightening effect that is given to it by the use of the
same language to describe her ultimate pauper's grave.
An obvious, theatrical trick, one would suppose, but it
succeeds. Again the horror of Gervaise's death is led up
to by those other deaths of the poor – Maman Coupeau
and Papa Bru. The little note of gaiety in Gervaise's

character in the days of the laundry's success which is shown in her simple power to amuse by imitation is to have horror in its sequence when she earns a drink or two by mimicking her husband in the padded cell. Coupeau's fear of drink, because his father, also a builder, had fallen to his death when drunk, is strangely fulfilled in reverse when his own fall leads to a convalescence that turns him into a drunkard. The two great humorous scenes in a novel full of a terrible ironic humour are neatly balanced in detail – the wedding feast and the feast of Nana's first communion. Though the whirring of the mechanism still distracts us on occasion in *L'Assommoir*, in *Germinal* and the later great novels it has been reduced to a ticking which enhances the reality of the atmosphere on which it has ceased to obtrude.

If the nervous undercurrent in Zola's life was made manifest spasmodically by mental obsessions and delusions, it was evidenced throughout his life by a physical hyperaesthesia which, like his obsession with numbers, is another great corner-stone of his creative powers. He saw, heard and, above all, smelt his surroundings more intensely than the normal person. To judge from his work we would suspect it was many years before this excess of physical sensitivity was integrated with the rest of his personality. It was responsible for the development within him of a poet – not the derivative, Romantic imitator of his youth, but a poet whose detailed powers of natural description allied him more to the Parnassian school, and who converted the natural phenomena he felt so intensely into images and shapes that finally give this side of his work a close link with the Symbolists. But the first emergence of this poetry in his novels, for example the famous descriptions of the food shops in *Le Ventre de Paris*, 1873, of which the symphony of the cheeses became notorious, was in the form of interspersed, lyrical passages of considerable power but quite unintegrated into the body of the novel. He attempted to overcome this technical difficulty by relating each 'food poem' to a particular character in the book, but the device is clumsy and did not solve the problem any better than the relation of the famous descriptions of hot-houses and aquaria which accompany the various steps of Renée's affaire with Maxime in *La Curée* (1872). These interpolated, ornate prose poems, repeated in the description of Paris in *Une Page d'Amour* (1878), look forward to work like Huysmans' *A Rebours*. Zola was to develop a means of using his poetry which was a far more remarkable technical achievement.

There was, it would seem, at the outset of his career, a barrier between the general, acute observation which went into the ordinary 'Realistic' narrative of his novels, and the more immediate violent accesses of aesthetic reaction which found their expression in the prose poem passages. The first was always informed with intellectual control, checked by carefully collected observations from outside sources, subordinate to the narrative and the formal demands of the novels. The second was a more powerful, concentrated, almost intuitive observation, which, however apparently disconnected with the surface theme of the novel in hand, had for Zola a deeper, more subconscious relation to it. Certain sounds, smells, sights would strike a response in him which made them a total pictorial symbol of the general theme on which he was engaged. This aspect of Zola's creative ability may perhaps be best compared with the active discipline of memory which Proust in his 'madeleine' passages makes the basis of artistic creation. It was not with Zola, of course, a conscious process, and in any case was less reminiscent than immediate. Proust, with his natural distaste for the dogma of Naturalism, seems never to have seen the extent to which his most cherished gift was shared by Zola; like so many critics who were misled by the stated Naturalist creed of Zola's school, he saw only a pedantic and ridiculous subordination to realism. If Zola had been forced to rely upon the more intellectually controlled observation which was the basis of the main narrative of his works, he would have been no more than such critics declared him, an academical realist painter, a sort of lesser Courbet. This is the competent level which he reached in some of his early novels – *la Fortune des Rougon*, *La Conquête de Plassans* – in which the influence of Balzac is less assimilated, the likeness to minor, realistic writers like Champfleury most marked. But the great lyrical descriptions of *La Curée* and *Le Ventre de Paris* already pointed to a wider, more original achievement, and by hard work and discipline he achieved the fusion of the surface and deep levels of observation which made him the great 'black poet' of *La Terre*, the great impressionistic realistic novelist of *Germinal* and *La Débâcle*, the Manet of despair.

The first steps towards this fusion can be seen in the publication of the first of his idyllic novels, *La Faute de l'Abbé Mouret* (1875). In this near fantasy of the young priest Serge Mouret's natural, Rousseauesque love idyll in the ruined garden, Zola attempted a whole novel drawn from his 'poetic' side. Effective though much of it is, the strain placed upon the fancy, the violent momentary imagination, by sustaining it at such length, was too great. Much of the book seems forced and laboured, nor was he to attempt such a thing again except in the short failure *Le Rêve*. But in order to give shape to the Abbé's tragic story he was forced to fill it in with a picture of village life that was drawn from his more immediate powers of observation. The possibility of fusion realized, the gates were opened that could let the fairy Ninon into the black, sterile world of the Rougon-Macquarts. The result of this union was the first of his great novels, *L'Assommoir* (1877).

In this, in many ways the most brutal of his works, the poetry has been diffused over the whole in symbol, humour, above all in the creation of a special language which fills the story of Gervaise with a peculiar fanciful character,* and yet seems only to heighten the realistic horror of the theme. The language spoken by his Parisian slum-dwellers was criticized then and since on the grounds that it was long since out of date and even then inexact. This justifiable charge was partly due to the naïve academicism which allowed Zola quite contentedly to take 'life' from dictionaries and text-books. But the charge is really irrelevant, for however outdated the argot Zola so transforms it and weaves it into the book that it flows over from the speech of the characters into his own narration. This, perhaps, was excessive, and he did not attempt it again, but in this general fusion of his poetry by symbol, humour and language he had found the colour with which to paint his great impressionist canvases. Each of the great novels was to have its own groups of words, partly symbolic, partly colouring, which recur in ever-changing patterns and varying intensity, like the dominating hues of a Monet or a Whistler.

This desire to give a predominating colour to each novel had, however, a certain danger. It encouraged the rather naïve academicism which has already been noticed. Zola's conscious adherence to realism, though fortunately

* It may be compared to the masterly language invented by Dickens for such characters as Mrs. Gamp.

swept on one side by the unconscious force of his creative
needs, made him preternaturally anxious concerning
correct detail, and his inferiority feelings about his
education increased this desire to be scholarly and exact.
Zola down the mines, in the fishmarket, riding with the
engine driver, talking to retired tarts, writing notes on
his cuff at bankers' receptions, the whole character of
the militant Naturalist on the warpath, according to the
Goncourt receipt, is a well-known figure. In part, it
belonged to his somewhat ill-judged publicity campaigns,
but in part it was his genuine method of approach to his
material. As the notebooks show, only a small proportion of the vast information he amassed was used,
but even so, it often stuck together like indigestible,
undercooked lumps in a pudding, obstructing the easy
flow of the narrative, upsetting the careful proportions
of the form. This was particularly common with details
derived from books or Government reports, for which
Zola had especial reverence. The description of the gold-
smith's work and of the forge in *L'Assommoir* are examples, as are the medical details of anaemia in *Une
Page d'Amour*, the information about seaweed in *La
Joie de Vivre* and almost the whole of the organization of
Paris finance in *L'Argent*.

More satisfactory, but still often insufficiently assimilated, were the symbols frequently drawn from the
animal world which are used to generalize the narrative.
The fat satisfaction of Mouton, the ginger cat of *Le Ventre
de Paris*, the continual frustrated maternalism of Man-
ouche, the cat of *La Joie de Vivre*, the strange life of the
pit ponies in *Germinal*, the mating of the cattle and the
birth of the calves in *La Terre*, are examples of this means
by which Zola reached towards and eventually attained
a content within his novels over and above, indeed

eventually more important than the history of the personages who appear in their pages.

The whole history of the Rougon-Macquart is the development of a detailed, realistic canvas into a statement of a mood, an atmosphere of a certain place and time within the same limited confines. It is as though Frith's 'Derby Day' broke and dissolved into a vast pattern of colour, sound and movement like some gigantic peopled Monet. Zola's earlier novels, however, for all their detail and precision are never static like the realism of Frith, his later panoramas never totally abstracted, sheer moods like Monet's scenes. Some critics, indeed, objected to the obtrusion of an individual character in such novels of mass movement as *Germinal* and *La Débâcle*. The crowd is the hero of such epics, they declared, and the formal narrative of individual lives only dissipates their force. But for Zola the crowd and the leading personages were one and the same, each was needed as the expression of the other. He could not even make the division into chorus and characters that Hardy did, though there is a great similarity between such profound melodramas as *La Terre, The Return of the Native, Germinal* and *Far from the Madding Crowd*. He was largely conscious of this movement of the focal point from individuals to groups, groups to institutions, institutions to the mass and the army, but he knew that the strength of his work lay in the pouring of huge vats of new material into the frames he had moulded so carefully and so long. Such changes of shape as were needed would come from the sheer force of the impact, not from a destruction of the old forms or a conscious search for outlines in which to encase an ocean.

Changes of shape were, however, constantly battered

out as the great wave of new ideas – institutional cross currents of jealousy, mob anxieties and hopes, the strange intuitive telegraphy and the hysteria of speculators or armies – poured in. But however overwhelming the flow, Zola still saw his work as single pictures and it was this formal discipline that gave his vast conceptions their artistic supremacy.

The wider the field and the louder the vibration of the mass overtones to his individual themes, the more strict the limits he imposed upon his picture. It is not surprising that he hankered after success as a playwright, for it was exactly the theatre's conventional limits of time and place, its external observation of character, its customary climaxes that were the source of his success. The author of *La Joie de Vivre* or *La Bête Humaine* might well have expected to do the work of Ibsen, but he could only have achieved such success by continuous development of his symbolism and such development could only have been at the expense of his unique verbal impressionism. It has been said more than once that Zola's great novels are the forerunners of the epic cinema – of D. W. Griffiths, of Jean Duvivier or of Pabst – but excellent films though many of them would make, such a view ignores the fact that Zola's greatness lies in his use of words. He was a pictorial artist, but to say that his world would be better represented by the camera is the result of an age-old confusion of means and results in the arts.

His inclination towards unity of time and place within individual novels is almost as marked as the homogeneity of tone and language by which he built up the atmosphere of each fictional world. He often held to such formal unities against the demand of realism. The natural climax which history contributed to his great series by the fall of the Second Empire in 1870 imposed upon him, in fact, a longer time scheme than he had in fact originally planned. The most striking example of such enforced change, of course, is the setting of Jean Macquart's war adventures in the Franco-Prussian War of 1870 rather than in the Italian campaigns of 1859 and 1860, but many of the other original schemes were equally affected. The treatment of *Nana* for which a dramatic ending was provided by the departure of the army from Paris in 1870 as the courtesan is dying, illustrates Zola's distaste for broken or prolonged time schemes. The death of Nana is in many respects a less successful climax than might be expected. This is partly due to Zola's curious choice of smallpox as the fell disease instead of the obvious syphilis, but it is also the result of the shadowy, unsuccessfully managed disappearance of Nana from the Paris scene for some years before she returns to die. These years of absence are necessary to the realism of the total time scheme as the fall of the Empire dictated it, but the break in continuity seems to have meant a break in Zola's intensity of interest. He naturally preferred a short and compact time scheme for, as in many of the great nineteenth-century novels, his characters, as we shall see later, did not develop.

If the unity of time which he tried to preserve in face of the demands of realism was a handicap, his unity of locality was a source of strength. Only by confining the movements of his characters was he able to build up the overpowering, inescapable atmosphere, the sense of hopeless imprisonment by which he holds the reader. Each class of society, each group of characters is shown within its own district, the very buildings and streets of which seem filled with the clashes of will, the frustrations of lust, the hopeless, creeping decay of the lives within them. For the poor this geographical prison is a symbol not only of their submerged lives but of their ignorance, the isolation to which the prudence of society has consigned them lest their infection should spread. From it they emerge – Gervaise's wedding party wandering round the Louvre, the strikers in the luxurious home of the manager, the peasants visiting the lawyer's office – like medieval voyagers to the land of Prester John, bewitched, awed, suspicious, and finally tired and bewildered. For the middle classes the locality is often, and purposely, I think, even narrower. It is the prison of the home – fat, prosperous, self-satisfied and treacherous like the well-filled shops of *Le Ventre de Paris*, stifling, priest-ridden, threatened by the undercurrents of hysteria and insanity, like the house of François Mouret in *la Conquête de Plassans*, rent with close-quartered hatreds and infidelities like the apartments of *Pot-Bouille*, or sunk in the muds of despair and melancholy like the Tchechovian home of *La Joie de Vivre*. The hopeless idylls of *La Faute de l'Abbé Mouret* and *Une Page d'Amour* do not leave the confines of their forbidden gardens. Even the rich suffocate in their overfurnished, overheated rooms as Renée and Maxime are overpowered by the force of their incestuous passion bred of ennui. Only in *L'Argent*, one of the last of the Rougon-Macquart novels, does Zola forsake his early expressed determination not to move from one section of society to another in the same book. The result is a confusion and a dissipation of energy which make this book, for all its greater cleverness and wider sympathy, one of the weakest of the series. We are already looking forward to that failure in power, bred of a greater liberality of emotion, which will be described in the account of the series *Les Trois Cités* (Chapter VI). Once, however, before the great creative impulse finally died in him, Zola managed to survey a wide scene with something of the intensity of his earlier novels. The army of Napoleon fights and retreats across vast areas of the East of France, but nevertheless *La Débâcle* does not fail to hold the attention as does *L'Argent*, or the post-Rougon-Macquart novels. In fact, the adventures of the broken, disillusioned French army, the final climax of hollow cruel comedy of the Second Empire, are for Zola an extension of the bewildered mood of Gervaise and her fellow revellers as they wander among the treasures of the Louvre and the whole novel is largely sustained on the note of prisoners released for an unhappy moment into a wider world from which they only long to return to their prison that has now fallen in pieces behind them.

If Zola's presentation of time and place supplies some key to the compulsion of his novels, his treatment of character gives the final answer. Zola was intensely interested in the physiological, medical approach to the human personality which the science of his youth propounded; one may well believe that the theories of Jeannet or Bergson would have attracted him as much as they did Proust, or that the views of Freud would have dominated him as they have later novelists. It is, however, very difficult to imagine a Freudian Zola, far more difficult to conceive a Freudian Flaubert or Tolstoy, let alone a Freudian George Eliot, Dostoevsky or Stendhal. As we have already noted, Zola began, like Dickens or Balzac, with characters that were largely humours. If he developed them, it was not by the enlargement of intellectual or emotional sympathy as George Eliot did, but by the unconscious infusion of his own personality into them. The Impressionist approach which he used could have led to a development of the interior monologue, as it did for Tolstoy, or to the tracking of memory as it did for Proust, but Zola's impressionism remained entirely fictional and external. Only one aspect of personal psychology really interested him deeply – the human will. It was probably this interest that attracted him to the works of Stendhal, at that time a neglected writer, and it is this interest that is predominant in his two 'psychological' horror stories, *Thérèse Raquin* and its later counterpart *La Bête Humaine*.

For the rest, character was for him merely a part of the general statement of his novels. Starting with a Balzacian realist approach, which was never entirely happy, he developed his humours in two directions; the central characters tended to be hardened into symbols, the others dissolved into 'humanity', crowds, groups. The family chronicle in the hands of most writers has tended to become a series of novels dominated by certain characters; indeed, the weakness of the later novels of many such family chronicles is that they are vehicles for developing some individuals with whom the author has become obsessed, addenda on Soames Forsyte, the Thibault father or Judith Herries, which are without shape as individual works of art. For Zola such an obsession, usually the mark of second-rate writers, was an impossibility. The simple 'humour' might gain force and energy as a symbol as Nana dominates her world, otherwise there can only be multiplication of characters to fill out the theme of the novel. Such a treatment of character is, of course, most successful where the world is a simple one, and it is for this reason that Zola's novels on the poor are his greatest. There are no more characters in *Pot-Bouille* than in *Germinal* or in *Son Excellence Eugène Rougon* than in *La Terre*, but the middle class and ruling class worlds demand a sophistication of character which, if it is granted, confuses, and if it is not, fails to convince.

Central characters exist in all his novels, but they are a convention like the much advertised tenets of naturalism which he only supported one moment to deny the next. The approach to the scene is always external, and if that external viewpoint is sometimes for the sake of convenience labelled Gervaise or Étienne, the scenes in which they are present merge happily and easily into those in which they are not: the observer is always Zola's five senses. The characters grow in number and in intensity, but never in intricacy, until, at last, in *La Débâcle*, they have dissipated into a vast, bewildered nation, through which move two moods, or symbols – despair labelled Maurice, and solid French character in whom the future lies – Jean Macquart. It was only when the long-planned series was ended and the long-sustained impulse flagged, that a dominating character appears – Abbé Froment of the trilogy – and with this domination of personal beliefs and anxieties comes a dissipation of energy which is marked by repetition, moralizing and ill-digested theory.

Chapter IV

THE YEARS OF SUCCESS

Biography of writer in adult years less important than
childhood – nevertheless conditions impetus of imagination – Dangers of certain aspects of success – Methods
of work writer's only weapon against attendant circumstances – insistence of Charpentier – Domestic circumstances – Death of Zola's mother – Jeanne Rozerat and her
influence – Social life of Zola – His taste – His entertaining – The Goncourts – Madame Charpentier – The
Academy – Flaubert, Turgenev, Daudet – The publicity
aspect of Zola's career – *Le Roman Expérimental* – Disciples
– Huysmans – Maupassant – *Soirées de Médan* – Manifesto
of the Five – Zola and the Theatre – Discipline of his work.

THE events, the circumstances of a great writer's
youth must claim the attention of the literary
critic who attempts to unravel the tight ball of
emotional strands from which the finished works receive
their pattern. Upon the stresses and strains, which fuse
the personality in these years, will depend in great
degree not only the force of the liberation of the ex-
plosion which gives the imaginative expression its power,
but also the vitality, the degree of nervous endurance
which is demanded by the hours and days of hard work
and patient drudgery without which no such incessant
demand upon the imagination can survive. The achievement of the great nineteenth-century novelists under the
demand of continuous and serial production, the only

road to large financial return, may perhaps be explained like that of the best sellers of our own century by the impelling wish for success and power which competitive society can produce in men of exceptional imaginative gifts. Demand for recognition may express itself in a series of 'great' novels as easily as in a series of 'great' political moves or 'great' financial coups. This is, in the main, the history of the major successful novelists of our own as of the preceding century.

But if will to success alone can produce, it cannot create, and unless sheer output is to take the place of creation, there must also be a deep fund of imagination, a reservoir of fancy to draw upon. It is a failure of this nature which separates the novelists of our own century, who worked within the old forms – Bennett, Galsworthy, Jules Romains, Dreiser, Thomas Mann. They lacked those vast childhood reserves with which their predecessors had filled their vast bottles – reserves upon which Dickens drew with greater results in each of his novels; reserves which, despite various declines, sustained Balzac and Dostoevsky to the end; reserves which only began to fail George Eliot at the close of her life; reserves which upheld Proust alone of the twentieth-century novelists – it is this which so closely allies *A la Recherche* to the work of the preceding century – throughout his long work, and then, only because he made them the conscious theme of his work; reserves which lasted Zola from his first conception of the Rougon-Macquart novels in 1867 until the completion of the last, *Le Docteur Pascal*, in 1892.

To understand the deep springs of Zola's work, it was necessary to discuss his early years in some detail; biographical events of his later years may, however, be considered more summarily.

If, however, the formative years of nineteenth-century writers are of vital importance to the understanding of their work – the explanation, it may be suggested, of the peculiar success which Marxist-Freudian literary biography has enjoyed in the study of that period – the general circumstances of a writer's adult life cannot be entirely neglected. In childhood and youth the armaments are amassed upon which victory or defeat depend, but the most powerful armaments may go down before difficult terrain. When the battle is engaged Zola's terrain was the fair upland of success, which has its deceptive bogs and morasses; he fought in a continuous and growing deluge of money, under which so many noble and confident captains have been buried. Above all he fought in the heart of competitive literary life and the fact that his name was mentioned daily in despatches only served to increase the suspicion and dislike which lay behind the congratulations of his colleagues – the smiles of Goncourt, the hearty backslap of Daudet. It was easy for so ambitious, so basically unsure a man as Zola under such circumstances to see all fair weather as a forerunner of storms.

Success, riches, literary esteem, the admiration of young writers, a secure and prosperous home life were, of course, the spoils for which he was fighting, and to speak of them only in terms of obstacles would be absurd. Without their promise he would not have attempted his great literary enterprise; without their background of security, ease and luxuriance he probably could not have succeeded in it; but within them lay pitfalls and against such pitfalls even the great force of pent-up creative need, which Zola's childhood happiness and adolescent misery had accumulated, might well not have prevailed had it not been for the exacting discipline of method and routine which he constructed in the writing of his novels. Before discussing the individual books of the Rougon-Macquart series, it is necessary, then, to examine some of the main aspects of Zola's life from 1871 to 1892, and to describe shortly the mechanics of his working methods.

Zola had already said goodbye to failure and squalor before 1870. His marriage to Alexandrine, his move to Batignolles – the prosperous Right Bank suburb – his small garden, his pet rabbits represent the first steps in the bourgeois ladder he was determined to climb. He returned from the Midi in 1871 to find the chaos and confusion of the Commune. For a time even the manuscript of his unpublished novel *La Curée* was missing. Then, to his horror, the government of the new Republic, from whom he had hoped at least neutrality towards his picture of the corruption of the Second Empire, suspended the serialization of his new book in *L'Aurore* on moral grounds. Portrayal of the decadence of high society could not, it seemed, be excused by ascribing it to the fallen régime. Shortly afterwards his publisher Lacroix went bankrupt. But for a stroke of fortune, Zola's career might have been thwarted at a vital moment. It was to Théophile Gautier, with whom he was not acquainted, that he owed his salvation from disaster. If his literary contemporaries were jealous of him, he received much from the Romantics and Parnassians he had rejected. Mendès and Gautier were important planks in Zola's career. Gautier urged Zola's cause to the young and enterprising publisher Charpentier, who took on the Rougon-Macquart series and remained Zola's publisher to the end of his life. It was a fortunate adoption for Zola; not only was Charpentier a clever and 'modern' publisher, but he was – a more rare phenomenon in this sphere – an exceedingly generous man. His original terms took full account of Zola's circumstances, his need not only for subsistence, but for expansion, and, as Zola's success grew, he saw to it that the author's share of the profits increased proportionately. Such generosity and foresight were, of course, not unrewarded. It was, however, particularly happy for Zola, since his original terms with Lacroix had been harshly wrung from him in his days of need, and had they continued, might have condemned him to profitless drudgery. Freed, then, from the financial nightmare of Scott's life or the intermittent warfare of Dickens' relations with his publishers, watched over by his wife and his publisher, Zola was able to become a very rich man and remain largely innocent about the management of money. A combination which, while it remains successful, may be regarded as charming in an artist, but which must be accounted pretentious, if it meets with disaster or dishonesty.

It was, perhaps, peculiarly fortunate that Zola's domestic life should not have been subjected to the additional stress of money worries. The emotional scenes, the neurosis and the despair which the Zolas were able to carry from one more splendid house on the Right Bank to another, moving ever inwards towards the Parc Monceau, were productive at least of the dark tragedy of *La Joie de Vivre*. In more indigent circumstances the sterility of his marriage might have dried up Zola's creative powers altogether. Alexandrine was a good, affectionate wife, a sensible housewife who retained her bourgeois thriftiness without cheeseparing, a friendly hostess, and a proud if somewhat ostentatious social companion to a rising author. If the greatest deficiency of the marriage – its childlessness – was hers, it was her

tragedy as much as his. That lack of children proved as
serious as it did was the fault of his temperament rather
than hers. Without being mother to his children, she
could only be the androgyne companion of his childhood
idylls – a part which by physique and character she was
quite unable to fulfil – or minister to his needs as his
mother had done before her. It was Zola's great failure
that he insisted upon providing his wife with an under-
study in the home in the person of his real mother.

For many years both women's devotion was sufficient
to smother the rivalry, but eventually it flared up into
rows and recriminations. Alexandrine was nothing if not
autocratic in the control of her household and the position was aggravated by the disposition of the Auberts –
Zola's mother's family – to borrow money from their
rich relative. Some years before her death Madame
François Zola ceased to live in her son's house, although
she continued to reside nearby. How bitter Madame
François Zola's hatred must have been may be seen from
the fancies and imaginings of her last illness. This event
which took place in 1880 was of great emotional significance to Zola and something must be said of its circumstances. Madame François had been on a visit to
relations at Verdun, where she fell ill, but insisted on
returning home. She was in fact seriously ill with heart
disease and the oedema which so frequently attends its
last stages. It was the daughter-in-law who, finding her
in a state of collapse following the journey, took her
down to Zola's country house at Médan. Alexandrine
nursed her in the last days. In the weakness of her physical condition, Madame François' fear and hostility towards her daughter-in-law welled up into suspicions and
charges of poisoning. Zola's fear of death was, in any
case, pathological, but the death of his mother, and in

such circumstances, brought to a head all the morbidity which he normally fought to express in fiction alone. It was one of the serious crises of his life. *La Joie de Vivre*, which he was writing, was postponed, to appear four years later with the circumstances of his mother's death incorporated in it. After long irresolution, he found his usual relief in work and it is notable that the result *Pot-Bouille* was a cynical, bitter attack upon bourgeois marriage as a cover for adultery.

Such sudden revelations of the black terrors that underlay his marriage, of which the events of his mother's death were only a peculiarly violent example, broke out again and again during these years of growing success. It is typical of the simplicity, which was the obverse of his suspicious fears of his friends, that he should have confided some of this inner life to Edmond de Goncourt. It was to him that Zola told of the wakeful nights in which he and Alexandrine lay weeping, neither questioning the other, for they knew that each was thinking of death and their failure to leave their name behind them. Such a story might well appear a malicious invention were it not confirmed by episodes in *La Joie de Vivre*. At another time, he was overcome by obsessions of the noise of wings of birds, and at yet another, by semi-hallucinations. Deep-seated neuroses of this kind might have been avoided had Zola's relations with his wife been more unequivocally hostile, but of their devotion to one another there can be no doubt – a devotion which each deserved. Suppression of antagonism was the only course, and neurosis the obvious result. For him the relief lay in the exhaustion of work, yet one can only gauge the discipline that such a remedy involved. For Alexandrine there was a more complete absorption in household management, and after the purchase of the estate at Médan in 1878, a devoted attention to local charity. This was a social expedient peculiarly unsatisfactory to Zola's generalizing mind, and with what a mixture of admiration and ironic amusement he followed his wife's labours may be seen in the brilliant and moving comedy of Pauline's efforts to rescue the half-savage children of the fishermen in *La Joie de Vivre*.

Such a domestic situation could have but one end for a man who was able to relax only in the company of youth and who needed an heir so fiercely. Once again, in 1887, it is Goncourt who tells of Zola's confession that he was more and more obsessed by the attractions of any passing pretty girl. It was in 1888 that he fell in love with one of the laundry maids at Médan. Jeanne Rozerat was then twenty. It was not long before she was established in a separate establishment and in September 1889 their first child, Denise, was born, to be followed by a son, Jacques, in September 1891. Zola had none of the conventional morality that could easily accept a 'second establishment'. Promiscuity was the symbol of evil and, more particularly, of failure for him. His relations with Jeanne and his children became a second, a happier, a more important marriage. The immediate effect, of course, was to bring the underlying tension of his life with Alexandrine into open warfare. Much has been said of her tempestuous fury on discovering the liaison, that she smashed a desk in her determination to find Jeanne's letters, etc. There were certainly violent scenes and for a time Zola's home life was a private hell. Yet it is difficult to see how she could have been expected to have assimilated the new situation more easily, unless her devotion had been more fragile. Her eventual recognition of the children and her attempt to incorporate them into her life with Émile strike a note of real, if pathetic, greatness of spirit; and there is something a little revolting in the half-grudging praise which Denise Le Blond-Zola gives to Alexandrine in her life of her father. If Madame Zola allowed herself a little theatricality in her public adoption of the children after her husband's death, in her declaration that a man of genius has his own laws, it was a small self-indulgence in a generous action. The only excuse for Denise's equivocal attitude must be found in the deep devotion that Jeanne inspired in all who knew her.

Zola, in fact, was remarkably fortunate in his choice which, guided as it must chiefly have been by a desire for youth, might well have been disastrous. Jeanne's effect upon his life and work was of major importance. She gave to him that simplicity and freedom from analysis in which alone he could be happy. In this atmosphere he was able at last to relax from the discipline of work, laze and taste in a more mundane form the strange 'natural' life which he had imagined in the Paradou scenes of *La Faute de l'Abbé Mouret* – at last he had found sex in which was neither sin nor death, a Paradise without the tree of knowledge or an avenging angel. The gradual slipping away of fears and horrors meant a decline in the need to sublimate their expression, although there was enough 'black poetry' left to fill the remaining volumes of the Rougon-Macquart series. Nevertheless, physical fatherhood was undoubtedly the precursor of literary sterility. *Le Rêve*, the novel of purity and beauty, is a forerunner of the novels of his last years with their elevated positive messages and their debased literary worth. It is probable that some such decline in literary greatness, some such assertion of the need for positive social expression would in any case have eventually overtaken Zola – there are marked weaknesses and repetitions

in the novels after *La Terre*, published in 1887 – but
Jeanne's gift of children and happiness hastened the
process. It is said that she was directly responsible for
giving his moral outlook, if not a more socialist expression, at any rate a more actively social form. Once again,
it may be said that *Germinal* shows this process to have
been already in action, but his natural pessimism and his
determinist reading made him obstinate in the rejection
of Utopianism. Intelligence alone might have led him
to a Marxist standpoint, towards which certain passages
in *L'Argent* suggest an inclination. At Jeanne Rozerat's
door then must be laid something of the emotional
benevolence of his final Fourierist views. On the other
hand, without her influence his need for social action
might well not have ripened by the time that he learnt
of the injustice to Dreyfus and so added a second great
fame to his achievement as a writer. With the best novels
of the Rougon-Macquart already given to the world we
cannot grudge the greatness he then showed in action.
Jeanne Rozerat must receive her credit in thus freeing
him for a new nobility and a new fight.

The personal contentment and calm which Jeanne
Rozerat brought to Zola, however, were not his until
fifteen of the twenty Rougon-Macquart novels had already
been published. The years of growing success and world-
wide fame were passed without the solace of real sexual
satisfaction or the contentment of children. These years
from 1871 to 1888 brought upon him the full strain of
the intensive work which alone could satisfy his violent
creative ambition. If he got comfort, care and, for considerable periods of time, understanding companionship
from Alexandrine, they could not in the circumstances
be enough to save his ravaged nervous system from
collapse, if there had not been other external outlets

for his desires and emotions. Success brought great wealth, and with it the possibility of indulging his generosity and his personal taste; it brought, too, the possibility of social life, in the narrower sense, and of the honours attached to it; it brought companionship with the great literary figures of the day; and, more importantly, the homage and affection of younger writers. None of these external outlets for Zola's sociable and affectionate nature, however, proved in the end to be more than palliatives, each was accompanied by tribulations, hostilities and jealousies which only increased his loneliness, his fears and suspicions. If there were ease, luxury and lavishness to cushion the appalling burden of continuous writing, they were the only unmixed blessings; for the rest he had to rely upon a life of vigorous discipline to canalize the powers within him and resist the drain of his emotion in external cares.

The volume of wealth brought in by the serialization of his books and by their subsequent manifold editions reached a height with the publication of *L'Assommoir* in 1877, and though many of the subsequent novels were less successful, the peak was largely maintained. It was fortunate that this was so, for Zola's expenditure, despite his wife's 'good management', must have been very large. He moved successively to smarter and richer apartments in Paris, and after the publication of *L'Assommoir*, he purchased the house at Médan on the Seine, which was to become so famous. He filled his houses with objets d'art of every kind, as would any of the adventurers from the Midi whom he satirizes in his own novels. The indiscriminate vulgarity of his personal taste forms a curious commentary on his early appreciation of the Impressionists. There is no doubt that he understood the work of Manet, because he saw in it a correspondence to his own literary ideals, but when he consciously expressed his taste in art, he fell into the worst excesses of indiscriminate richness and display which satisfied his taste for profusion and colour. In his artistic tastes, as in his intellectual views, he was behind the times rather than with them. When the chic mode of Art Nouveau was spreading its etiolation and spare elegance like its beloved pomegranate vine over the smart houses of Paris, Zola was still cramming his rooms with disordered masses of medievalry, French Renaissance, fake antique and Oriental. Busts of Venus and Antinous jostle against ivory carvings and richly bound missals, Japanese screens and fans (some with the inevitable erotic themes of the millionaire household) vie with Sèvres vases and carved bureaux of the François Premier era. It must have been for Zola a supremely satisfying indulgence of childish desires, and for his fashionable visitors an occasion for exactly that polite and elegant amusement which he was always ready to suspect.

At least, however, he could fill the house with people, and still find seclusion in which to carry out his work. From his earliest, most impecunious days on the left Bank, Zola had loved parties. With each successive move in the social scale his hospitality became more lavish, the circle of friends wider.

Zola's own love of good food and drink was inordinate. Apart from the famous gastronomic feasts at Parisian restaurants* which he shared with Flaubert, Turgenev, Daudet and Goncourt, there were Sunday dinners at Flaubert's house and Thursday dinners at Zola's home, whilst the regular fare which Alexandrine supplied was

* The first of the famous dinners at Trapp's Restaurant which received wide newspaper publicity took place in 1877.

on a generous scale. Good living and sedentary habits
gradually changed Zola from the elegant, feline young
man of Manet's pictures to the gross figure whom the
caricaturists of 1880 loved to depict with a Rubensesque
tart 'Nana' on his knee. The change in his appearance
eventually began to worry Zola himself, and he adopted
a more frugal diet, with little wine,* and that, never
with his food. It was this diet that turned him into the
spare academic figure with beard, pincenez and bicycling
knickerbockers who rode the country lanes so happily
with Jeanne Rozerat.

Much has been made both in his lifetime and since of
Zola's changes of friendship. It is surely inevitable that
a man whose interests and social position changed so
rapidly should lose old friends and make new. For the
ordinary ambitious man, whose happiness lay in the
present and not the past, such changes would have
occurred almost imperceptibly and without pain at any
rate to himself. But for Zola, with his childhood fixation,
the loss of old friends was a painful process. Already, before the Franco-Prussian war, he had begun to grow out
of touch with the Aixois circle in Paris. To them, for
whom success was still a dream, Aix was always a centre
of discussion, if only to abuse its narrowness and boast
of their indifference towards it. Zola's revenge on Aix
was already taking literary shape, and after the publication of *La Faute de l'Abbé Mouret* in 1875 it begins to fade
from his books as from his mind. The interests of the
little Provençal group lay predominantly in painting, his
were increasingly literary.

His first attempt to extend his social life had been a
failure, for he was soon cold-shouldered by the Meurice

* His English translator, naïve, puritan, Radical Vizetelly, was
thus happily able to speak of him as 'almost a total abstainer'.

group who ran *L'Appel*, when they found him to be a critic of their idol Victor Hugo. The contact with the Goncourt brothers, which followed their interest in *Thérèse Raquin*, and more importantly Zola's praise of their work, was of far greater moment than any inclusion in a die-hard Romantic clique. The relationship was ultimately to be as unhappy as it was important, particularly after the death of Jules de Goncourt. For Edmond, the constant eclipsing of his own fame by that of the young provincial whom he had hoped to patronize, became steadily more intolerable; and a subterranean warfare, for which Goncourt was much better equipped than Zola, raged incessantly between them. In the early years, however, all was fair, though there is a certain equivocal note even in the first entry about Zola in the Goncourt diary – Dec. 14, 1868. 'In short, not a little modelled in his own person after the characters of his books, those complex beings, sometimes almost female in their masculinity.' A perspicacious description, but not the one most friendly to Zola's own point of view of his public character.

From a social point of view, the connection with the firm of Charpentier was to prove as valuable as it was financially profitable. Madame Charpentier, a young, attractive, smart woman, held a salon in which Zola rapidly became the leading figure and in which he came into contact with a fashionable world that was so essential to his novels. Though she was never to acquire the significance that Madame Caillavet had for Anatole France, Madame Charpentier gave that element of smart flirtation and wordly counsel to her relation with Zola, that is an essential part of the histrionic make-up of many artists. It was she above all who urged him to demand the honours that were his due from the bourgeois society which he attacked. It was she who obtained the Légion d'Honneur for him in 1888. It was she, also, who encouraged him to present his name for election to the Académie Française in 1890, when Daudet's name was among the candidates. Zola never obtained entry to the Académie, though he continued to present his name every year for election. This belief that he should insist on justice against all prejudice and hostility is a clue to the difference of outlook between him and the other great writers of the day. What to him was a proper demand for recognition was to them a lack of pride, and they counted it as part of the general self-advertisement which they found so embarrassing in his career.

Even Flaubert, whose semi-paternal status amongst the naturalists allowed him to remain aloof from much of the bitterness, often expressed his private disgust at what he regarded as Zola's public antics, and even on occasion reproved him personally. If Flaubert, with assured fame, found Zola's tactics for public recognition graceless, it is easy to see how they were seized upon for censure by Goncourt and Daudet, whose popularity and sales were being eclipsed. During the 'seventies, when Flaubert was still present to enforce good behaviour by the strength of his personality, the meetings of the four novelists were outwardly amicable, and there is no doubt that Zola gained greatly from the opportunity of exchanging ideas with men of his own calibre. The presence of Turgenev, too, not only gave Zola a Russian market* for his work which was the start of his European reputation, but also restrained hidden enmities before a distinguished foreigner. Flaubert's criticism of Zola's work, it is true, grew towards the end of his life, as he

* Much of Zola's work, particularly his literary criticism, was published in the *Vyestnik Yeuropi* before publication in France.

felt greater suspicion of the younger man's campaigns to force 'Naturalism' upon the public. Such crude systematization was alien to Flaubert, and, even more so, the idea of popularizing literary theories. Their affection, however, was still strong enough to make Flaubert's death in 1880 a serious blow to Zola in that dark year of his mother's death.

The 'publicity campaign' aspect of Zola's literary career which pained Flaubert and gave ammunition to Daudet's and Goncourt's jealousy was, it is true, a purely designed affair. Zola had saved himself from starvation by journalism, and he never lost the journalist's flair for the sensational. As his individual novels with their revelations of social degradation were forced upon society by their violence, so, in some degree, his whole career was a stampede, in which shock tactics were an important element.

But there were emotional needs that Zola satisfied in these campaigns which his rivals could not perceive. If they were isolated and lonely as he was – as indeed most artists must be – they accept it resignedly; for Zola, with his spoilt-child nature, such resignation was impossible. He must force the public to take his works even if only by abusing them. In addition he must present his artistic method as though it were a solid intellectual scheme, lend that air of culture and education – of which in reality he knew himself deficient – to present as a logical theory what was in fact the form in which his individual genius expressed itself. The most extreme attempt at such intellectual disguise was his publication of *Le Roman Expérimental*, in which he attempted to find an analogy between the determinist physiological theories of Dr. Claude Bernard and his own approach to novel writing. There are few literary manifestos of such poor quality and Flaubert was rightly horrified at its appearance. It is perhaps not altogether strange, that this attempt to defend literary objectivity in terms of scientific determinism should have been published at a time when we may suspect that Zola was first beginning to feel the need of some positive creed beyond artistic expression and, perhaps more important, when his disciples were openly moving towards other forms of literary expression.

The importance to Zola of leading a body of literary opinion was also unintelligible to Flaubert, who, if he liked the admiration of younger writers, did not wish to marshal them into a school of imitators. For Zola his disciples were, perhaps, the most hopeful avenue of escape from his loneliness and insecurity. When he lost touch with Baille, Cézanne and Roux, they took with them most of his beloved boyhood. Any hopes he may have entertained, that the young Provençal Valabrègue would prove a new link to the scenes of the past were soon shattered, when the young poet returned to seclusion in the Midi against Zola's advice. The appearance of his first admirer, the faithful Paul Alexis, in 1869, is then an event of great importance in Zola's life. Alexis, alone of the group that gathered round him, remained faithful to the end, writing the master's life as early as 1882, and encouraging his children to play with Jeanne Rozerat's. Of the rest of Zola's disciples, Hennique and Céard continued to write in the Naturalist tradition, though they eventually lost touch with him personally.* The two most eminent of his followers – Huysmans and Maupassant – were to follow quite other

* Céard, who was his favourite, was closely connected with the beginning of his liaison with Jeanne Rozerat. But the quarrels between Émile and Alexandrine, of whom he was also very fond, eventually drove him away.

roads. The height of Zola's happiness as master of the much advertised Naturalist School was reached with the publication of the *Soirées de Médan*, a collection of short stories, to which all the disciples and the master contributed. The title of the collection was a tribute to the hospitality and gaiety of Zola's country home, and serves to remind us that the unhappiness of his existence threaded its way through a life of genuine pleasure. The collection was published in 1880, otherwise a black year for Zola. By an irony the great success of Maupassant's *Boule-de-Suif* set him only more firmly on the independent career that led away from dogmatic Naturalism. Huysmans, too, was soon to depart into the fashionable neo-Catholic Symbolism, which was to become a red light to Zola for the corruption of the younger generation.

It was into this atmosphere of parting ways and dissipating loyalties that the famous Manifesto of the Five was hurled. It is impossible to charge Goncourt or Daudet with complicity in this document, but their disclaimers do not carry complete conviction, and there is no doubt that they welcomed the action of their protégés in publishing it. The manifesto, which appeared on the front page of *Le Figaro* on August 18th, 1887, purported to express the disgust of the younger generation at *La Terre*. Since none of the signatories was a friend of Zola – they were indeed disciples of Goncourt, some of whom had recently been staying with him – their victim was able to make light of the matter. But the terms in which it was cast and the moment of its appearance cannot but have wounded him deeply. Reference was made directly to his childlessness and to his wealth. The growing obscenity of his works, it declared, 'Some have attributed to a malady of the lower organs of the

writer, to the mania of a solitary monk, others to an
unconscious development of a passion for sales.' 'We
are convinced', it ended dramatically, 'that La Terre is
not the momentary stumbling of a great man, but the
accumulation of a great series of downward steps, the
irremediable, marked depravity of a chaste man.'
Bonnetain, the chief signatory, it must be added, had
written a novel Charlot s'amuse which was a study of
masturbation. The real disciples all rallied round Zola
in face of this attack, but the fact that, for some of them,
the rally was a public rather than a genuine expression
of feeling can only have brought home to Zola the fact
that his methods were becoming out of date. It would
probably be true to say that his liaison with Jeanne
Rozerat healed as serious a wound in filling the place of
his young disciples as it did in providing him with
children.*

If, on the surface, then, his life in the years of the
creation of his great novels appears almost the crown of
success – wealth, home life, great brother novelists,
followers – examination shows each blessing in a less
rosy light. Not a little of his love of public favour, his
almost childish delight in interviews with journalists
and foreign visitors – George Moore, de Amicis and

---

* That a certain latent homosexuality—the female side of the
androgyne idyll—fought for expression whilst he was childless seems
probable. Towards overt homosexuality his attitude is difficult to
determine. He was only dissuaded by his friends, who feared for his
reputation, from including a novel on the subject in the Rougon-
Macquart series. But this may well be explained by his desire to complete the picture of Second Empire social life. It is less easy to explain
his letters to Dr. Saint Paul in 1895 asking him to lend his name as a
medical man to the publication of an anonymous manuscript Roman
d'un inverti. On the other hand he refused to sign the petition got up
for Oscar Wilde.

others – his much advertised submission to physiological examinations as a genius, the whole circus aspect of his career may be attributed to the insufficiency of his private affections. Much of this exhibitionism diminishes after 1886 and his own histrionic part in it found ample scope in the events of the Dreyfus case, as his opponents were quick to point out.

He might well have expected to find a more immediate public affection in the world of the theatre than he could realize in the vast anonymous public who read his books. Here, indeed, he met with ill luck. The scope of the present study does not allow for a detailed study of his plays, but while they are not on a level with his best novels, they are not incompetent and made a real departure from the stereotyped French stage traditions of his day. In plays like *Les Héritiers Rabourdin*, in which he acknowledged a debt to Ben Jonson's *Volpone*, he attempted a new realism on the stage which may be compared to the contemporary revolution being carried out by Ibsen and Tchechov. Such French dramatists as Bernstein and Brieux, indeed, owed a direct debt to him. Unfortunately the power of cliques in the Parisian theatre was enough to kill the early performances under circumstances of considerable humiliation to the author, and although the adaptions of his novels, particularly after he acquired the collaboration of Alfred Bruneau in 1888, met with greater success, his unpleasant experience dissuaded him from ever participating in the public performances.

It was not, then, through external public sympathy that he could find the strength to carry out his gigantic task, but by discipline and absorption. Each novel was prepared by months of careful reading, examination of locales and witnesses, by general absorption in the milieu which he intended to portray. Much has been written against this approach to creation, which has been attacked as academic and 'unfelt'. The romantic fallacy that imagination can only derive from 'lived' experience will be more fully examined, when the essay of his most recent critic, Dr. Lukacs, is considered with the Marxist objections to *Germinal*. Here it can be noted that whatever the artistic value of such an approach, its personal absorption and discipline were a very important aspect of Zola's defence against the intrusion of his private anxieties upon his creative process. Finally, when all the ground had been prepared, he subjected himself to a rigorous programme of work from nine in the morning until eight at night with a short break for a meal. Such was the harsh routine which made possible the 'high project'. 'Journalism has rendered me a service', he told Goncourt. 'It has taught me how to work. In the old days a kind of surplus of ideas and theories would, at a certain point, choke in me and cause me to throw up my pen in despair. Now there is a regular flow, a less abundant current, but freed from encumbrances', and again, 'Don't think I have much will. I am by nature the weakest and the most subject to distractions. Will has been supplanted in me by the fixed idea which renders me sick if I do not yield to its obsession.'

Chapter V

LES ROUGON-MACQUART:
A SUMMING-UP

Zola's novels for the English reader – grouping of the
Rougon-Macquart novels – origins of the Rougon-
Macquart family – The Aix novels: *La Fortune des Rougon,
La Conquête de Plassans* – *Le Docteur Pascal* – The Idylls:
L'Abbé Mouret, Une Page d'Amour, Le Rêve – Autobiographical
novels: *La Joie de Vivre, L'Œuvre* – *La Bête Humaine* –
The Social novels – ruling class novels: *La Curée, Eugène
Rougon, Nana, L'Argent* – Bourgeois novels: *Le Ventre de
Paris, Pot-Bouille, Au Bonheur des Dames* – Novels of the
People: *L'Assommoir, Germinal* – Zola and the Masses –
La Terre – *La Débâcle.*

ENOUGH, perhaps, has been said of the general
nature of the Rougon-Macquart series, and of the
circumstances in which they were composed, to
make discussion of the individual novels meaningful
even to that considerable number of English readers of
nineteenth-century literature for whom Zola is still
largely a name. It is only perhaps in a few – *L'Assommoir,
Germinal, La Terre,* perhaps *La Débâcle* – that Zola can
claim to rank with the very greatest novelists of his century. There are, however, many more – *La Curée, Le
Ventre de Paris, La Faute de l'Abbé Mouret, Nana, Pot-
Bouille, La Joie de Vivre, La Bête Humaine* – which are both
more outstanding as works of literature and more readable as narratives than many of the Victorian novels

which have acquired 'classical' status in the general re-appraisal which our longing for assured standards and established forms has given to the fiction of the last century. The unfortunate circumstances attaching to the first translations of Zola's work in England* have meant that only poor and condensed translations of his works have been available to the general public. Complete translations by writers of standing have been issued solely in limited editions.† A recent and excellent translation of *L'Œuvre* as 'The Masterpiece' by Thomas Walton, though an unfortunate choice of a dull book, points the way to a happier state of affairs. Meanwhile, at a time when the second-hand shelves of booksellers are frequently empty, copies of Zola's novels in the original French are still to be found in cheap profusion. There is, then, little excuse for continued neglect of his work in this country.

While any detailed statement of the plot of the Rougon-Macquart series, either as a whole or within the single volumes, would be both tedious and outside the scope of this study, a short preliminary statement about the origins of the family may help the reader to understand better any details of narrative which may be needed to describe the individual novels. Tante Dide, the foundress of both the Rougon and the Macquart families, was born before the French Revolution, and survives as an old paralysed and speechless woman into the pages of the

---

* The story of Henry Vizetelly's trial and condemnation for publication of obscenity as a result of his son's translation of *La Terre* in 1888 is a long and interesting story, but it formed a fog of 'smuttiness' around Zola which has not yet completely dispersed. (See Appendix.)

† The exception is Havelock Ellis' translation of *Germinal* available in the 'Everyman' series.

last novel, the events of which take place shortly after
the fall of the Second Empire. An orphaned and hysterical young girl with a small property, Dide marries a local
peasant, a hard, tenacious, acquisitive man. From this
union are sprung the Rougons who descend upon the
upper ranks of Second Empire Society in Paris and evidence in their fierce, calculating, predatory hunt for
wealth and position both the retentive brute force of
their peasant ancestor, and the wasteful, lustful power
of their crazed déclassée ancestress. Dide later becomes
the mistress of a lazy, cruel, poaching tramp, the outcast
of the little peasant society of Plassans; a man whose
intelligence, superior to his environment, has been
turned solely to getting what he wants on easy terms.
There are two children of this union – Antoine and
Ursule. From Antoine, a village scrounger whose sole
difference from his criminal father lies in his determination not to meet a violent end, descend the great proletarian stock of the Macquarts. For them, too, the gor-
geous Paris of Louis Napoléon acts as a magnet, but their
ambitions and lusts are sucked away into the drains of the
city's slums by the easy way and the immediate pleasure.
Nevertheless from them are born the hopes for the future
– Étienne, the revolutionary, and Jean, the sturdy peasant who returns to till the soil and breed future generations. Ursule Macquart by her marriage to Mouret, the
prosperous Marseilles tradesman, produces the third
group: the bourgeois adventurers, who thrive upon the
decay of the old Parisian middle classes, to create the
great new monopolist tradesmen. From Ursule, too,
are sprung the provincial bourgeoisie, in whose close,
jealous family atmosphere the hereditary madness and
lust take strange, shut-in, manic forms. The permutations
of so wide a network are manifold, and, as has been said,

allowed the novelist full scope to write as he wished. The complicated scheme of physical and mental inheritance, which Zola set forth in the genealogical trees he issued from time to time, became of less and less significance as the work proceeded. Nevertheless the family chronicle framework had great use in giving form and shape to the vast onrush of ideas with which Zola was first assailed. Without its seeming limitation, he might never have dared to face his task. Apart from this subjective value, too, it must be admitted that the vision of a wandering brood, sprung from a tainted stem, burrowing and fighting its way through the shaking structure of the glittering Empire has a violent and dramatic quality which again and again returns to strike the reader, when, absorbed in the course of some independent narrative, he would think himself most remote from the family drama.

In general, however, the novels stand as separate works of art. Their strength, as has been stated, lies in their evocation of a total atmosphere, what in psychoanalytical discussion of dreams is often called the 'affect'. If a detailed discussion of the novels would be otiose, some attempt to suggest these peculiar 'affects', if only for the greatest of the novels, seems worthwhile, as part of an appreciative and evocative approach to Zola's work – an approach which is perhaps the most valuable task that literary criticism can perform. Since the novels have already been viewed as part of a general biographical scheme, a chronological consideration would prove repetitious. In the following discussion, therefore, the novels have been grouped into six or seven main aspects. The first written and the first considered are those dealing with Aix or Plassans in realistic description or satire. The next are those connected with the boyhood idyll, beginning with the 'black idyll' of *La Faute de l'Abbé Mouret* laid in Provence, passing to the grey Paris idyll of *Une Page d'Amour*, and ending with *Le Rêve*, the pure 'roman bleu'. The boyhood idyll worked out, we pass to the directly autobiographical novels *Le Joie de Vivre* and *L'Œuvre*. *La Bête Humaine*, which is discussed next, connects with the pre-Rougon-Macquart novel *Thérèse Raquin* and lies close to a personal fantasy of Zola, though in general setting it might be ranked with the novels of working-class life. Finally we may deal in turn with the novels of Second Empire high society, politics and finance; with the bourgeois novels of professional life, monopoly retail trade and small shopkeepers; and with the novels of working-class life – both the Marxist term 'proletarian' or the nineteenth-century expression 'life of the poor' might distort their meaning – which include Zola's four greatest works.

When the series was first conceived, Zola was still much absorbed in his contempt, his desire for revenge upon his native Aix; and Plassans, its fictitious form, is the scene of three of the earlier novels. After *La Faute de l'Abbé Mouret* (1875) however, in which Provence is only secondary to the theme of the doom of natural sexual love, he had largely worked his childhood out of his system, and Plassans does not reappear until the threads of the whole series are somewhat artificially, though dexterously, gathered together in the last novel *Le Docteur Pascal* (1893).

The first and fourth novels of the series contain the main force of his attack upon Provençal society. Though neither are among his failures, and indeed may still be read with pleasure as competent works of the type of the early French realist School of Champfleury, their main interest lies in certain particular features of Zola's genius which are an essential of his great novels. *La Fortune des Rougon* in which the family history is set, shows the impact of Louis Napoleon's coup d'état upon a provincial town. Zola's basic contempt for the liberal Republicans appears in his treatment of the futility of the popular rising and the hypocritical use of Republican ideas by Antoine Macquart, the cunning wastrel, to secure any plum that might fall from the shaken tree. His essential compassion for those who truly espoused the liberal ideals and were sacrificed by the incompetence or roguery of their leaders is apparent here in the moving episode of the execution of the gaping peasant who is shot by the Bonapartist troops, because it is too troublesome to break the manacle that ties him to the young hero Silvère. In Silvère's love story appears, as has been said, the first portrayal of the ill-fated adolescent idyll. The local intrigues, in particular the meetings in Félicité Rougon's yellow salon which becomes the Bonapartist centre, are treated with the broad irony which he was to use with such mastery in describing more elevated scenes of social ambition and political manœuvring. The whole book shows the influence of Balzac's provincial novels in a somewhat undigested form. It was, however, remarkable enough to gain the author congratulatory letters from Flaubert, Gautier and Goncourt.

In *La Conquête de Plassans*, published three years later, Zola uses the Provençal scene in the first of his attacks upon the Church. He returned to the anti-clerical theme in *La Faute de l'Abbé Mouret*, but hostility to the Church was not to dominate his work until the *Trois Cités* trilogy which followed the Rougon-Macquart series. *La Conquête de Plassans* shows the Church at the moment when she has finally decided that Louis Napoléon's régime is firmly enough established to be a useful ally. An ambitious priest of peasant stock is sent to the village to make sure that the local Bonapartist clique of Rougons are properly directed. His establishment as a tenant in the house of the prosperous, old-fashioned radical rentier François Mouret provides Zola with the double theme of the dangerous, hysterical power of the priesthood and the strange, insane roots that lie beneath the complacent, comfortable flowering of bourgeois domesticity. With the exception of *La Bête Humaine*, which is more success-ful because of its frankly horrific nature, *La Conquête de Plassans* is the most melodramatic of the series. Marthe, François Mouret's wife, changes from an honest, mater-nal bourgeoise to an obsession-ridden hysteric, whose religious madness is carefully fostered by the priest; while François himself is driven insane by his jealous fears and, prowling like a beast on all fours, sets fire to the home, which is his god. That we should be fascinated, if not convinced, by such melodrama is a mark of that growing impulsive force which is Zola's most individual gift. A remark from his notes about Marthe reveals the simplicity of his assumptions – 'She falls into religion. That's enough to explain all that follows. From the moment she becomes dévote, she can go off the rails in any way you like.' Yet exactly that simple assumption controls the book, and largely convinces the reader. It is interesting to note that *La Conquête de Plassans* was pub-lished in the same year as Barbey d'Aurévilly's *Les Diaboliques*, which Zola attacked so fiercely for its melo-dramatic improbability. As the growth of irrationalism and neo-Catholicism isolated Zola from the fashionable thought of his day, he opposed their 'melodramatic improbability' with scenes of melodrama almost as improbable, yet always more convincing and more real because of his simple and clear view of the structure of society from which no fin-de-siècle weariness or terror of social change could shift him. *Le Docteur Pascal*, the last novel of the series, published in 1893, returns to Plassans after the collapse of the Empire. It would hardly be fair to criticize it as a work of art on the level of the other nineteen, for its main purpose is to tie up the loose ends of family chronicle, and with the birth of a child to Clotilde Rougon by her uncle Pascal to point a somewhat lurid finger towards the hopes of future generations. Curiously enough the same note of wild but arresting melodrama marks the work as *La Conquête de Plassans*, an inevitable element, perhaps, of the geographical scenes of the author's childhood. There are two immensely powerful and impelling scenes in the death of the drunken old Antoine Macquart from internal combustion in the blazing sun, and the slow death from haemophilia of the beautiful degenerate boy Charles Rougon before the paralysed old, old foundress of the line, Tante Dide, who, startled into hysteric life, gives out a last cry. Something of the combination of irony and melodrama in which Zola succeeds so eminently may be illustrated by the circumstances of Antoine's death – 'It was the finest case of spontaneous combustion that a doctor had ever seen – nothing remained of him, not a bone, not a tooth, not a nail, nothing but a little heap of grey dust which the draught from the door threatened to sweep away'. Yet this same bragging, atheistical old rogue Antoine has left all his money for a magnificent tomb, described in all its details of nine-teenth-century, Gothic horror. The executors could only gather together a general heap of rubbish 'in which very little of their uncle could remain', and they are forced to ignore the terms of the will. The main interest of *Le Docteur Pascal* lies in certain autobiographical elements which will be considered in relation to the change in Zola's outlook which occurred in the last years of his life.*

The only other Provençal novel is *La Faute de l'Abbé Mouret*. Enough has been said of the general erotic theme of this book in the foregoing chapters. It is the only novel in which this theme of the natural adolescent sexual idyll, with its strange androgynous sensuality, is played out as the central plot. It is only here, in the old childhood settings, that he allows himself to reveal his fantasy as a sympathetic 'natural' love; whenever it is directly stated elsewhere, it is seen as a decadent accompaniment of the lives of the vicious and sated rich. Even in *La Faute de l'Abbé Mouret*, Serge and Albine have their Paradise not in the rocky countryside, but in a vast overgrown artificial garden, the fancy of an eighteenth-century libertine run wild, not far different from the hot-house tropical setting of the parallel but vicious idyll of the hectic, pleasure-weary Renée and Maxime of *La Curée*. On the surface, the book is an attack upon the sterility of celibacy and gives in the Friar, who chases Serge Mouret from his artificial Paradise back to his duties as a priest, that picture of the clergy driven forward by a maniac hatred of sex that is almost a Manichaean detestation of the human species, which Zola was to develop in the novels of his last years. Nevertheless, if Serge is punished for listening to the voice of the Church, by the pitiful death of Albine and her child, it is impossible to imagine how the boy-girl idyll could have continued, once the child – beautiful chance result of the onrush of loving impulses – had been born, and one must suspect that Zola also punished, if only un-

* Chapter VI.

consciously, the ultimate sterility of his fantasies in this tragic ending. The lush and ornate love story is, however, most beautifully, if occasionally somewhat self-consciously, conveyed. It is interesting to note that, if it worried realists like Champfleury, it delighted Catulle Mendès and Massenet. Perhaps it was this lush note that disturbed Renan, who otherwise might have been expected to welcome so moralistic an attack upon organized religion. It was the only work of Zola that he read – 'It's too long', he said, when interviewed, 'too long, yes, a little long. Oh! he's a fine man certainly. – It's not fully written, it's not worked out – it was done too quickly, that's clear. But, well, he's certainly a fine man'.

Une Page d'Amour (1878) has as its theme Zola's favourite idea of bourgeois marriage in its loveless, false atmosphere as the incentive to adultery. Here, however, the adultery is treated as sympathetically as a genuine search for idyllic love – once more in a wild Paris garden – by two lonely people. The widowed Hélène Mouret's transgression upon the married sanctity of her neighbour is punished by the death of her hysteric, invalid little girl, whose jealousy of her mother's love for a stranger is too much for her fragile frame. The picture of this precocious, yet tyrannical child is brilliantly carried out. The sister of Little Nell, or Lise in *The Brothers Karamazov*, Zola treats her without Dickens' or Dostoevsky's sentimentality; and if her death is a punishment for her mother's adultery, it is also perfectly clear, from Hélène's subsequent marriage and departure from Paris, that Zola has no illusion about the morbid, anti-social nature of precocious, invalid children – little Dolls' Dressmakers – in an adult world. For the rest the work is remarkable for a series of Monet-like

impressionistic sketches of Paris seen in various lights
which are neither good in themselves nor absorbed into
the book. Conceived as a conscious antidote to the
popular outcry at the blackness of *L'Assommoir*, *Une Page
d'Amour* is better than its determinedly beautiful nature
might have made it, or than Zola's own fears suggest –
'C'est un peu popote, un peu jeanjean', he wrote to
Huysmans – and it contains one passage of combined
lyricism and irony, a description of a rich bourgeois
children's party, which is among his finest pieces of
writing.

If this grey idyll escapes the charges of maudlin pretty-
prettiness which he feared, *Le Rêve* (1888), written to
dispel the baneful effects of *La Terre*, cannot be excused.
The unreality of its pseudo-simple, pseudo-medieval
atmosphere shows Zola at his most artificial and looks
forward to the worst excesses of 'simple beauty' in his
last novels. One can only feel satisfaction that this
unusually timid attempt to gain favour with the conventional should have failed. Anatole France rightly declared that the attempt had been made only at the cost
of all merit. It is interesting, however, to note how often
this novel is selected for special praise by those to whom
Zola's work is repugnant, but who yet feel the need to
acknowledge his greatness.

We may now pass from the novels in which Zola's
fantasies are directly presented without attention to the
dictates of realism to those novels in which fragments
of autobiography are directly presented in realistic
settings. *La Joie de Vivre* (1884) is an overflow of the
deeper personal miseries which were usually absorbed
into the objective analysis of his novels. It is this sur-
charge of personal bitterness, with its inevitable undercurrent of self-pity, which prevents *La Joie de Vivre* from

being Zola's greatest novel, flattening out its form and reducing it to a shapeless, yet brilliantly written chronicle of human failure and slow decay. Like so many 'near misses', it has to rank among its author's failures; yet viewed as a bitter comedy of man's neurotic failure to use his gifts, it may well rank with Tchechov's plays. So many diverse streams of Zola's unhappiness run into it, so much self-punishment is combined with so much self-defence, that we may well marvel at the final impression or depression of unity which it presents. Already conceived before his mother's death in 1880, the breakdown which followed that event caused him to postpone its writing. In its final form the work is a retribution to Alexandrine, and, yet also, a rejection of her sterility, and a bitter attack upon the protective, the fiercely adoring love which his mother had given him. The character of Lazare, the central male character, a gifted young man, spoilt and enervated, who drifts from one enterprise to another but will not leave the rotting nest, is primarily an expression of Zola's bitterness against the dilettantism, the neo-Catholicism and decadence of the younger generation. 'Un René ou Werther naturaliste', he describes him in his notes, a Huysmans who has rejected his master, we may guess. But in a deeper sense, it is an expression of his own fears of dissipated energy and failure, and he seeks, in self-defence, to put much of the blame on the suffocating love of his mother.

The powerful effect of this little, bourgeois household, decaying from intelligent, happy activity to bitter, stale emptiness in its setting of a remote, poverty-stricken seaside village, is hard to convey. We see the mother as a cheerful, humorous, active woman, a little too fond of her son, a little too house-proud, gradually turning to a lying, cruel tyrant, as she devours little by little the capital of her ward, Pauline, to finance her son in his successive failures, and then by a brilliant turn, this pervasive, tyrannical force is cut off by a failure of her wicked energy – heart failure and death. We watch Lazare, the son, drifting from one high concept to another failure in application. We are given the tragedy of his marriage for money to a pretty doll, a brilliant reverse of Dickens' Dora or perhaps an Isabella Linton, isolated on these storm-swept beaches as Isabella on the Yorkshire moors. Greatest tragedy, we are shown the sad fate of the heroine, Pauline – whose good sense, devotion and humour might in other circumstances have made her an Elizabeth Bennet – condemned to sterility and fruitless good works. In the background is the character of the father, a selfish invalid, whose will to live preserves him as a cipher among these people whose thwarted passions and energies are wearing them out. At the end, this old, useless, paralysed man cries, 'Kill oneself! How stupid! When life has so much to offer!' Every author has, perhaps, a magnificent failure which shows potentialities unrealized in his greatest success. *La Joie de Vivre* is Zola's wasted glory.

If *La Joie de Vivre* is broken by the overflow of the author's personal passions, *L'Œuvre* (1886) never comes to life because it is fed upon dead or superficial emotions. The general scheme of the Rougon-Macquart series was formulated at a time when Zola was losing contact with the Provençal group of artists – in particular Cézanne – who had been the friends of his youth. Claude Lantier, the artist hero of *L'Œuvre*, first appears as an incidental character in *Le Ventre de Paris* (1873) and the ideas he expresses in that book have more life than the whole of the later work. Zola, however, was always obstinately attached to themes, and he produced the novel about artists, when his feelings about the loss of his boyhood friend, once so strong, were almost dead. If any living emotions are embodied in the novel they are the suspicions and bitterness which were growing up between him and the Goncourt–Daudet world, but these were surface and more suitable to polemic than art. For the rest, the book has enjoyed fame as a supposed picture of Cézanne in the hero, though Claude Lantier represents as much a picture of Zola's own fears of failure as of his former friend. There is some incidental interest in the ideas he puts into the mouth of Sandoz, a confessedly autobiographical character, for they represent the picture he wished to present to the world. The whole book is clogged with talk about painting in which he was no longer interested. Ironically enough, the realist debunking of the Murger sentimentality about la vie de Bohéme was more satisfactorily expressed in Goncourt's *Charles Demailly*.

La Béte Humaine (1890) stands apart from all the rest of the Rougon-Macquart novels. The first projects had determined upon a homicidal maniac as the crown of the family's degeneracy, but Étienne Lantier, who was intended for the part, acquired a 'good' character in *Germinal*. Zola was forced to go back on all that had been said in previous novels and invent an additional son for the heroine of *L'Assommoir* – Pierre – to fulfil the predestined murderer's role. It has been already noted that the general theme shows the persistence of the strange guilt feelings that were associated with his wife's previous lover, which had been expressed in *Thérèse Raquin*. It is likely that the whole scheme might have been scrapped, had it not been for the impact of Dostoevsky's *Crime and Punishment* which aroused his enthusiasm. On the whole, although more popular, *La Bête Humaine* is a less successful treatment of crime and guilt than *Thérèse Raquin*. It is essentially a roman à thèse, and in its undisguisedly horrific nature, it departs more consciously from realism than any of its predecessors. Yet Zola seems not to have seen that this necessitated a different treatment. He had already projected a detailed novel on railways,* and he attempted to combine the two approaches. As a result, the ethical horror story, which required a simple presentation, is presented with all the fullness required of one of his great social novels and becomes over-involved with technical details, tangled guilt motives and double plots. In addition, he abandoned the idea of a pederastic murder at the last minute, as too revolting.† Nevertheless, *La Bête Humaine*, if a failure in its more serious aspect, is deservedly popular as a thriller.

We are now free to turn to the novels in which personal emotion has been transformed into zeal for social analysis; in which the personal conflict is only apparent in the social symbol or the general 'affect' of the social scene; in which this 'affect' or atmosphere is built up by a careful, detailed observation and framed by an exceptionally shrewd analysis of the structure of society. These are the Naturalist novels proper, the most typical of Zola; and they contain his greatest works.

The earliest of such novels to be published – the second in the Rougon-Macquart series – was *La Curée*

---

* His use of railways as a mise-en-scène and a symbol is far inferior to Dickens' many passages on them. Zola, of course, could not look back to pre-railway days, they had less mystery for him.

† It is characteristic of his refusal totally to abandon ideas that he used this theme ten years later in *Vérité* where it no longer has meaning and appears flat.

(1872). Here Zola, without any first-hand experience, plunges straight into the feverish, complicated world of the adventurer–speculators who formed the café society of the Second Empire. In this novel and in the next novel of high society *Son Excellence Eugène Rougon* (1876) in which he goes right to the heart of the Imperial power – the adventurers fighting for office around Napoleon himself – Zola suffered not only from inexperience of his subject, but also from insufficient technique to control the large stage and crowded dramatis personae which the many groups that made up the ruling class required. This weakness even persists somewhat in *Nana* (1880) and prevents it from taking its place with the four great novels of working-class life.

It is, of course, easier to suggest groups of simpler people, whose range of expression and coherence is still limited, than to sketch in similar bodies of more sophisticated or educated people, for whom assertion of individuality is the first claim to existence.

By the time that his mastery of technique was sufficient to deal with the complicated actions of the 'monde', as for example in *L'Argent* (1891), the last high-life novel of the Rougon-Macquart series, there is already a failure of power, a stale repetition of characters and situations which announces the decline of his powers.

If none of the novels about the ruling classes, however, is of the first rank, *La Curée* and *Nana*, at least, have a certain peculiar atmosphere of excitement and desperation which make them both unique. In later years, when Zola had entrée to great houses, he regretted that he had not known them when he was describing the receptions in *La Curée*. There is, perhaps, at first a feeling of unreality, of over-richness, about his descriptions, a suspicion of the eye of the servants' hall, which has been seized upon by those who know that he used the *Mémoires d'un valet de chambre* for the description of the Imperial Court in *Son Excellence*. Like Dickens, he has long been accused of knowing nothing of the aristocracy he satirized, of vulgarizing and missing the point. Dickens' satires of society, however, are now rightly admired. The Dedlocks, the Merdles, Mrs. Gowan, the Veneerings, Lady Tippins are regarded as among his triumphs. The same re-estimation should certainly be made for Zola. His brutal financiers, purple and apoplectic, as they pursue the high-class tarts who ruin them; his etiolated young men playing in boredom at affaires with ageing but still beautiful society women who are as frightened of time passing as they are bored with its presence; his respectable, upright politicians, obsessed by the worthless cheapness of some second-rate actress; the disorder and laziness, the unemptied slops and thieving servants that surround the vulgar, generous-hearted, mercenary demimondaines; all these may have a certain air of exaggeration, yet they are not so far removed from Odette and Charlus, Basin and Oriane de Guermantes that we can dismiss their truth. Provincialism* shows itself, it is true, in the rich profusion of the scenes of splendour and decay, for Zola's moral horror of waste was appalled at such spectacles of sexual energy dying in sterility and boredom, and his deeply sensual nature was as fascinated as appalled. Yet there is always an underlying irony, a grim and enlarged sense of the physical functions, which lie round the corner from physical beauty, that recalls Swift's pathological approach to women. The Nana who, on hearing that her ruined lover has made a funeral pyre of his own racing stables, cries extravagantly,

---

* A well-known man-about-town, Aurélien Scholl, said '*Nana* is a Parisian novel for provincials, but a provincial novel for Parisians'.

'That was a man!', is also the Nana who skimps and haggles over the price of the laundry. The lovely adventuress Clorinde, the desired of Eugène, lolls, serenaded by young poets, amidst unemptied bowls of dirty water and old hair ends. It is this harshly moral sense of the skeleton beneath the skin that makes Renée's feverish passion for her pitiless, pretty stepson in *La Curée*, and Nana's locust flight over her rich lovers, such horrifying and yet moving spectacles.

Despite his greater knowledge of society and his firmer control of his medium, Zola had ceased to see sex as the hideous alluring wasteful road to death when he came to write *L'Argent* in 1890. He had found sexual fulfilment in Jeanne and his children. The same themes are satirized, the same characters presented, and with more dexterity: there is less absurdity, less extravagance, but the old atmosphere of eroticism, as cloying as Delacroix in pornographic mood, as savage as Swift or St. Paul denouncing the flesh, has gone. The theme has no more meaning for him, the sterile idyll and the sterile nightmare are both dead.

The first novel of bourgeois life in the Rougon-Macquart chronicle, *Le Ventre de Paris* (1873) was the third of the series. Like *Nana* and *La Joie de Vivre*, it only just misses ranking with Zola's masterpieces. The failure of the other two, as of *Pot-Bouille*, lies in a general extravagance of treatment, a too-great monotony of savagery, despair or lust. *Le Ventre de Paris* has the variation and sense of proportion which belong to Zola at his best; it has also the exaggerated sweep without which he could write nothing good; it fails only from lack of technical mastery. It marks the beginning of many new aspects of the author's work which were to be essential ingredients of his greatest novels, but he was clearly uncertain how to handle them and the novel emerges as a fascinating but unintegrated collection of potentialities. The ornate flower imagery of *La Curée* had given some indication of that method of entwined symbol and realism by which Zola was eventually to convey atmosphere so brilliantly, but *Le Ventre de Paris* may well be called his first successful essay in impressionism. The choice of milieu was very wise. The vast organization of the Halles – the stomach, the markets of Paris – with its colours, smells and noises; the prosperous, fat, comfortable petite bourgeoisie of the small provision shops in the early days of the Second Empire before they were threatened by large-scale monopolists; the sleek, handsome, lazy Lisa Macquart with her benevolence to the profitable, and her smiling cruelty to those, like her idealistic brother-in-law, who threaten her secure pattern of life – these are themes on three levels which combine and intertwine to make up that impressionistic picture, part social, part moral, part sensuous, which was to be the pattern of Zola's great works. The famous symphonies of smells – descriptions of various types of food symbolizing the different aspects of petit bourgeois success – are perhaps a little ornate, they are certainly still too unintegrated into the novels and stand out as set pieces. The novel is overweighted with plots and characters; Zola is clearly bursting to say all that was to go into the next ten years' work. The comic plot and counterplot of the liberal conspirators and police agents, recalling Balzac's *Splendeurs et Misères des Courtisanes*, is over-involved. Claude Lantier's reflections on painting, the boy-girl idyll of the slum waifs Marjolin and Cadine fall over each other, and lead nowhere. Nevertheless, despite its faulty construction and overweighted plot, *Le Ventre de Paris* is a unique and absorbing novel.

It was not until 1882 that Zola took up his onslaught on the bourgeoisie once more with *Pot-Bouille*. It is, both in form and theme, one of the most peculiar of Zola's books; indeed, it can hardly be said to conform to any shape which even the flexible novel form had previously assumed. Confined almost entirely to one household of bourgeois apartments, it has the effect on the reader of a play. The constant amorous intrigues and adulteries of the 'professional class' characters recall the comedies of Wycherley, whilst the brutal and frank comments of the underpaid, corrupt servants upon the sex lives of their masters serve as a satisfactory chorus. The whole book could be most happily presented in the form of a bitter satire on respectable domestic life as a cover for promiscuity, shown on a stage that allowed for six or more compartments in which to play the various intrigues simultaneously. To Zola, 'arranged' marriages were the highroad to sexual squalor, whilst the romantic conceptions of love with which well-bred girls were imbued at their finishing schools were only a greater incentive to turn their loveless marriages into a succession of sad, little, pseudo-romantic adulteries. In 1881, in an article in *Figaro*, he wrote, 'If, among the common people, surroundings and education push girls into prostitution, the circumstances and teaching of middle-class women drive them into adultery.' It was natural that a novel which was solely concerned to illustrate this view in all possible permutations should cause an outcry, and it is, indeed, difficult to regard *Pot-Bouille* as a realist work, despite its lifelike characters and incidents; as denunciatory extravaganza, however, it is both very funny and very horrifying. Its publication was carefully designed to follow *L'Assommoir* whose sombre picture of working-class life had been so admired by bourgeois critics, and Brunetière, one of Zola's harshest critics, was probably right in declaring that its chief fault in the eyes of readers was 'lèse-bourgeoisie'.

Au Bonheur des Dames, the direct sequel to *Pot-Bouille,* in which the Provençal adventurer, Octave Mouret, climbs by means of the sexual desires of the bourgeoises of the earlier book to control of the greatest department store of Paris, has been among the most admired of Zola's works. Not a little of this praise is accorded to it because it was the first novel to have an institution, to which all the characters are subordinated, as its hero. We have suffered from so many hotels and shops at the hands of Arnold Bennett or, on a lower level, Vicki Baum, since then, that it is difficult to feel much enthusiasm for pioneer work in this field. It acted, however, as a direct inspiration to Jules Romains and others of the now moribund 'Unanimist' school. Even if the critic is prepared to accept the somewhat naïve idea that the routine functions of a large-scale organization present a ready-made artistic scheme, *Au Bonheur des Dames* presents a less satisfactory and living whole than the mining community of *Germinal* or the routed army of *La Débâcle.* Despite some excellent descriptions of the canteen back-biting of the underpaid shop assistants, *Au Bonheur des Dames* is perhaps the one novel by Zola that fits the often reiterated charge that he substituted careful, detailed note-taking about life for life itself. Apart from the relationship of Denise, the shopgirl heroine, to Octave, her employer, the rest of the book is worked up, if excellently worked up, Mass Observation. The careful resistance of Denise to Octave's advances and her triumphant emergence as his proud wife are all too like a 'Pamela' without Richardson's sensitive analysis of character. The humane staff-reforms which she demands as the price of her hand are a palliative to what might seem to be Zola's too great submission to the worship of success in his hero, Octave; they are also the first tentative statement of ideas of social co-operation which were later to flower into full blooming Fourierism. The dreary refinement of Denise's character hangs like mildew over the whole novel, though Zola himself in his notes makes it clear that he intended the work to be a gay, lively acceptance of 'things as they are'.

The four remaining novels of the Rougon-Macquart Chronicle – the novels of 'the people' – are his greatest. To attempt to convey the character of works that are in the first rank of novel writing in a few pages is an impossible task. The critics' most honourable course can only be to urge the public to read them; but some few notes about their peculiarities may perhaps act as an incentive.

With the publication of *L'Assommoir* in 1877, Zola leapt from extraordinary talent to a mastery of his medium that can, without distortion, be labelled genius. The theme had been maturing in his mind since 1869, and the most striking feature of the book is its deeply felt quality. The heroine, Gervaise, is perhaps the most completely conceived character, belonging to that great class of submerged, unindividual figures that make up the very poor, to be found in all nineteenth-century fiction. The tragedy of her limited fight – limited by education and circumstances – to win a pathetic little vision of individual happiness from an uncomprehended and uninterested world is treated with the greatest pity and the least false sentiment. In a note, Zola says, 'I must show all the world trying to bring about her ruin, consciously or unconsciously', and so we see it. Odd figures who are never mentioned again add to her misery and her failure by their petty tyranny or their failure to comprehend – an old woman shuts her window triumphantly as Coupeau, Gervaise's husband, falls from the roof he is repairing to become the lazy, crippled drunkard who destroys her hard-won prosperity; persons in the crowd laugh, as her somewhat ludicrous wedding procession – the summit of expression of beauty in her life – passes by; the warders at the Louvre in their superior uniform only make more awesome the glories of that mysterious exhibition, through which the little wedding party wanders in proud but ignorant aspiration towards dignified and higher pleasures. In these incidental figures we have the whole world of strangers, of the educated, of the busybody and the official who beset and tyrannize and make small the submerged when they attempt to rise above the surface. The simple demands of Gervaise and Coupeau upon life, their capacity for gaiety, their childlike hopes and dreams are all attended by little incidents or remarks that foreshadow their futility. On second reading, perhaps, the careful interlocking of the present hope with its future foundering seems a little careful, a little arranged, but, at first encounter, the effect of gradual, yet inevitable descent is overpowering. The tragedy and the horror would be unbearable – indeed a mere recapitulation of the events would make them ludicrous – if it was not for the concept of limited, pitiable, yet complete human dignity which marks Gervaise. It is perhaps almost unbearable, almost inartistic, when events finally reduce her human dignity to animal squalor – reality has outrun art. We may despise the bourgeois critics who shouted against the outrageous horror of *L'Assommoir*, but our special contempt must be reserved for those left-wing critics who did not find the picture of the submerged sufficiently noble. 'My characters', said Zola, 'are not bad, they are only ignorant and destroyed by the surroundings of crude need and misery in which they live.'

No account of *L'Assommoir* is complete, however, without mention of the humour of the scenes of prosperity and gaiety which intersperse the descent of Gervaise. Such humour is abundant in many of his books, but nowhere so successfully as in *L'Assommoir* and *La Terre*. The wonderful wedding visit to the Louvre is well known, as also the wedding feast; less famous but as good are the birth of Nana and the goose feast. The humours of ignorance and superstition, of the oddities of the simple have been surpassed only by Dickens – at Nana's cradle, her aunts dispute – 'Madame Lorilleux held that, to have a boy, you must turn the head of the bed towards the North, but Madame Lerat, shrugging her shoulders, called such an idea childish, and gave another receipt, which consisted in hiding a bundle of nettles freshly gathered in the sun under the mattress, without telling the pregnant woman', or again, 'as M. Poisson plunged the carving knife into the goose, M. Lorilleux had a sudden feeling of patriotism. "Ha! if that was a Cossack", he cried. "Have you fought against the Cossacks, M. Poisson?" asked Madame Boche politely. "No! with the Bedouins", replied the policeman, "There are no more Cossacks".' In such incidents we have all the pathetic humour of ignorant authority and inconsequential misinformation that play so large a part in the lives of the very poor.

If *L'Assommoir* moves the reader's compassion for the submerged through the individual life of Gervaise, *Germinal* (1885) uses the submerged community of the miners to compel his belief, if necessary, his hostile and frightened belief, in their right and their power to climb out of the hell to which indifference and greed have consigned them. If, in 1885, strike action was less rare than it had been when Dickens so sadly failed to grasp its necessity in *Hard Times*, it was still thought of by 'respectable' people as criminal violence. It was this aspect of bourgeois fear, this feeling that strikers were only collected criminals, violators of the sacred rights of property more vile than thieves because more dangerous, that Zola deliberately played upon. 'Il faut que le lecteur bourgeois ait un frisson de terreur,' he said. Nor could the reader take comfort in the bewildered failure of the strike; in the almost frivolous remoteness from reality of the deeply serious professional revolutionary leader Souvarine; in the remote and overwhelming power of the Kafka-esque 'they', the management in distant Paris; in the ruthless suppression by armed force and the return to worse conditions; for, as the hero, Étienne, leaves the mining town at the end of the book, he hears the tap, tap of the army of workers beneath the ground, and he knows that they will eventually cut their way to freedom. *Germinal* is rightly regarded as one of the greatest novels of the masses. Nowhere perhaps have scenes of mass action been more deftly managed, nowhere the confused emotions and thoughts of simple people, treated like beasts and driven into self-defence that is often bestial, more directly made lucid without losing reality. Zola uses all his devices, and less obviously than in *L'Assommoir*. The hero, Étienne Lantier, a stranger to the mining town, provides an observer for a community which has no self-consciousness. The building-up of that community through the lives of individuals makes a clear and detailed picture which later mass writers so often blurred by attempting to portray groups directly. Many left wing admirers, notably Barbusse, who have objected

to the 'intrusion' of individuals, have failed to see that
the force of compassion and anger which they praise
rests exactly upon this method. Nowhere, too, is Zola's
'journalistic' approach – his visits to mines, his interviews with working men, his notes, his reading of reports – more truly vindicated than in the great imaginative scenes underground, the descents in the cages, the
mining ponies, the flooded pits. It seems strange that
this should not have more completely convinced Zola's
most recent critic, Dr. Lukacs. In his brilliant work of
Marxist literary criticism *Studies in European Realism*, he
makes a penetrating and interesting defence of Balzac
and Stendhal as the great socially conscious novelists of
the nineteenth century. Zola, whom he admires for his
fight for Dreyfus, he rejects as a writer, chiefly on the
ground of his bourgeois, journalistic, unparticipating
approach to life. He claims for Balzac and Stendhal a
fuller degree of socially conscious participation, and
supports his view, in particular, by reference to their
large-scale archetypal characters – Julien Sorel, Vautrin,
etc. After the events of 1848, he suggests, it was impossible for a bourgeois writer to allow himself the same
degree of social consciousness, especially – a familiar
Marxist standpoint – a radical bourgeois of Zola's type.
This failure is chiefly shown in the 'smallness' of Zola's
characters against what he calls 'the romantically
rhetorical monumentality' of their surroundings, which
he compares to Victor Hugo's work. Such a discrep-
ancy, he argues, reveals the weakness of Zola's work, its
distance from social reality, and, he continues, there is
no greater revelation of that weakness than Zola's
journalistic method of work – his interviews and note-
taking, the summit of his non-participation. One cannot
help suspecting that, despite Lukacs' praise of Zola's

actions in the Dreyfus case, he is prejudiced against his non-Marxist, radical materialism in a way that he cannot be against the more 'realistic' reactionary views of Balzac. This prejudice has led him to seize upon Zola's journalistic method as an explanation of his failure, but, in so doing, he leaves his Marxist ground and falls back upon the old romantic fallacy that an author must 'live' his work. In fact, of course, an approach by notes and papers which is invested with a deep social imagination may produce work as socially convincing and powerful in its social illumination as the use of direct experience. It is not quite clear, either, why a post-1848 radical should not *unconsciously* reflect Marx's analysis of society as much as a reactionary of the 1830's – indeed, he allows Dickens, whose radicalism only differs in kind from Zola's, such unconscious powers. *Germinal*, more than any other of Zola's novels, seems to defy Lukacs' view; for despite the 'smallness' of its characters and the 'monumentality' of its setting, it declares and shouts the decay of the bourgeois system from within, and shows the *actual* power of the workers as opposed to any sentimentally conceded 'rights', like some personally felt and imagined illustration of the 1848 Communist Manifesto. Nevertheless, the method of its preparation – Zola's interviews with miners, talks with Socialist deputies, descents into mines – was the most journalistic, the most widely advertised that he ever employed.

L'Assommoir is Zola's most compassionate work, *Germinal* his most angry, but *La Terre* (1887) is the most complete of all his novels. In it are brought together all the various strands of emotion which had competed for expression in the other Rougon-Macquart novels; in it Zola combines and blends more happily all the various methods of expression which had been individually perfected in its predecessors. It is a book of incidents and characters, that taken separately are the height of his exaggeration, his monstrous view of life, yet, united and fused, are the summit of his truth, his convincing projection of reality. The 'Lear' tragedy of the 'hard' old peasant Fouan, driven from one brutal, calculating child to another; the insatiable greed by which no division of land can satisfy them, no sacrifice of the old man's patriarchal power suffice until they have dragged the last sou from his carefully guarded tin of savings; the horror of the scene in which his son-in-law – about the most understandable entirely wicked character of nineteenth-century fiction – disposes of the old man when he is finally paralysed and useless; the fierce, primeval figure of the old peasant woman La Grande tyrannizing over her brood with no greater weapons than a stick and the force of traditional superstition; these are the most striking examples of Zola's 'black poetry'. The peasants gathered round the lanterns at night listening to 'Jacques Bonhomme', the propagandist Imperial leaflet upon the glories of 'the soil' and the countryman's existence, their wonder as its lyrical panegyric unfolds, their failure to comprehend that this idyllic picture has any connection with their own hard fight to wring a few extra sous from the impoverished soil – 'si tu as la paix du cœur, ta fortune est faite' says the leaflet, and 'l'argent seul est bon' their hearts respond – this and other scenes have a Shakespearean force that only Hardy's peasant choruses have rivalled. Nowhere is Zola's comedy so successful as with the respectable M. and Madame Charles, whose chief pride is their sleek, demure, convent-bred granddaughter, yet whose source of income is the brothel of the nearby town. The scene, in which this innocent young lady is told of the sinister origin of her 'dot' and reveals that she is only waiting to take the establishment on so that more modern methods may produce greater profits, is a triumph of comedy. But *La Terre* achieves greatness, that is denied to many of the other novels as rich in horror and irony, by the truth, the simple nobility of the hero and heroine, Jean and Françoise, whose greater feeling and finer aspirations are so skilfully woven into the same pattern of external coarseness and callousness as the sunken, brutalized mass around them, that they give a final conviction of mankind's possible redemption in the most vile swamps. This sense of nobility in the lower depths of life can only be compared to the greatest successes of Dostoevsky in *The House of the Dead* or *The Idiot*.

To compare *La Débâcle* (1892) with the three great novels which have just been discussed would be to claim too much. Nevertheless it may certainly rank as one of the most successful war-novels ever written. The storm of abuse from army circles – precursor of the greater storm that burst round Zola at his trial – which followed its publication is some measure of its powerful anti-militaristic quality. It is natural that Zola's picture of the retreat and collapse of the French Army after Sedan should invite comparison with Tolstoy's *War and Peace*. This comparison is perhaps more valuable than it may appear at first sight. Tolstoy's work is, of course, on a far more epic scale, at once more broadly and more solidly conceived. Nevertheless their picture of moving armies as forces far beyond the control or comprehension of those who command and direct them, their emphasis upon rumour, superstition, baseless courage and baseless fear as the driving forces of great campaigns are essentially similar; their method of presentation, too, by disconnected scenes, individual adventures,

the spontaneous actions of small groups of soldiers and
'historic' meetings of great figures is directed to the
same end – the portrayal of 'chance' as the mover of
events, the explanation of this 'chance' as the unsuspect-
ed interaction of the historically 'petty' and the historically 'great'. By his suppression of character Zola is,
perhaps, superior in 'conveying' the gathering momen-
tum of the atmosphere of a bewildered, disorganized
fleeing army. For if *La Débâcle* lacks Tolstoy's great epic
characters like Pierre and Andrei, conceived with a
breadth and depth of which Zola was hardly capable, it
is also free from the vast interior monologues, of which
Tolstoy was one of the first great exponents; and skilful
though his technical use of this form of presentation was,
Tolstoy's narrative is inevitably bogged and slowed down
by it. Finally, if the main characters through whom
Tolstoy presents his panorama of society are on a scale
outside Zola's range, the contrast between the weak
intellectual, Maurice, the noble peasant, and Jean Macquart, in whom the events of 1870 are personalized,
shows that Zola was inclined towards the same distrust
of intellect and cleverness, the same faith in the traditional strength of the peasantry, to which Tolstoy also
came in his old age.

Chapter VI

LAST YEARS

Comparative literary unimportance of Zola's last years—
The formulation of positive social theories – the nature
of these theories – *Les Trois Cités* – artistic weariness –
Zola and the Church – Zola and the Jews – the Dreyfus
Case – Zola's trial – Exile and England – *Les Quatres
Évangiles* – Nature of the Promised Land – Zola's death.

With the completion of the Rougon-Macquart
series in 1893 Zola's contribution to literature was made. He was to design seven more
large novels, and complete six, but, if the earlier of these
are not without much of his old greatness, there is an
atmosphere of repetition and fatigue about them which
had already shown itself in *L'Argent*, whilst the novels
of his last years, though they remain a somewhat ludicrous monument to the moral greatness of his character,
can only be regarded as the ruins of his literary power.
Zola's artistic genius was the expression of emotional
and intellectual conflict. Peace came to his spirit with
Jeanne Rozerat and his children; intellectual solution
followed more slowly but was no less complete. Though
a lifetime of writing made it natural that he should seek
to express this final solution in books, its true expression
lay in action. The courage, the generosity and the force
which he showed in his defence of Dreyfus are the monument of these last years of positive conviction, they have
their place in the history of France and in the history of

human freedom, but they can only form a brief appendix to a study of Zola as a writer.

To introduce this appendix, we must examine briefly the steps which led to Zola's positive social faith, to what may well be called his 'conversion'. The most positive element in Zola's character may be said to be his love of life, though at times this assumed stronger negative shape in his neurotic fear of death. This passionate absorption in life is the key to his personal ambition, and his earliest positive affirmation, apart from his devotion to his art, is expressed in an acceptance of existence, of self-determination to survive and succeed which marks *Eugène Rougon* and *Au Bonheur des Dames*. Eugène and Octave are the types of Vitalist belief in the self, using circumstances and people to increase their power and to dominate their environment. Two facts, however, prevented Zola from remaining satisfied with this crude materialist 'hero' philosophy, both of which were forced into the open by his clear analysis of society. If *L'Assommoir* paints a black and hopeless picture of the working classes, the compassion that he felt for failure and defeat boils over in it. If he extends admiration to Eugène and Octave, he describes with deadly clarity the waste and muddle that were inherent in the class system by which they rose to power. It is not then surprising that in *Germinal* he should not only give compassion to the workers, but transfer to them the faith that he had formerly given to the superman. If only failure and defeat still attended their efforts to free themselves from slavery, he makes it clear that only in their eventual victory can a society be refounded which promises life for all, instead of death for the many, and power, which is no less a death, for the few. Moreover he accepts the necessity of violence to attain this end.

It is the nearest point that he reaches to revolutionary socialism, though in *L'Argent* he puts the Marxist analysis of history into the mouth of one of the most sympathetic characters. His own personal misery was too embedded in violence, his own need for love was too great to make him easily accept a positive violent creed. Darwinian determinism pointed logically to Marxist determinism, but once this became clear in the revolutionary socialism of *Germinal*, he began to retreat from determinism towards Utopia. His personal and sexual idylls had, as we know, always been utopian, and now he was also to seek to build the Garden of Paradise in society at large. The earliest evidence of this, perhaps, appears in the character of Jean Macquart in *La Terre*. This simple, traditional young peasant gradually sheds so many of the limitations of sensibility and understanding of his surroundings that, when he reappears in *La Débâcle*, it is his tenderness, his courage and his shrewdness which symbolize the living France. The neurotic fears and doubts of the intellectual Maurice are France's temporary death. It is notable that Maurice is the type of young neurotic whom Zola normally showed – for example in *La Joie de Vivre* – as neo-Catholic, anti-scientific; yet in *La Débâcle* by an anachronism he is made to join the Commune. The anachronism is extremely significant: Zola, as we know, in his young artistic days had found the Commune simply an obstruction to his career as a writer, now he paints it as the logical end of the rotten class system of the Second Empire. This is a clear renunciation of violence. It is with Jean, the traditional French worker, determined to cultivate his garden, that the future lies. Not, of course, that Zola deserted socialism or science, accepted superstition or social stalemate, but he rejected revolution. His old distrust of the liberal reformers of 1848 as windbags or the tools of reaction never left him, however. If revolution and liberalism were rejected, the only escape could lie in some form of non-violent revolutionary belief, an Utopian Socialism. The character of Docteur Pascal is important in this development. This was in some respects an avowed self-portrait, and the whole novel was dedicated to Jeanne Rozerat, who appears as the young niece-mistress of Pascal, Clotilde. Pascal dies a convinced materialist scientist, his work is destroyed by superstitition and bourgeois fear, but a child is born and it is with this symbol of the future that the building of the new world, the freeing of the life forces and the vindication of science lie. Pascal is old enough to have learnt the 'wisdom' of waiting: it may not be today, but wait, my friends, there is all time before us. Such wisdom, of course, lies deep in the heart of Zola's new-found domestic happiness, but it lies a little embarrassingly far from the compassion of *L'Assommoir* or the anger of *Germinal*.

Inevitably, perhaps, Zola began to be concerned not only with political Utopias – with Saint-Simon, Proudhon, Fourier – but also with faith. The Catholics who received the news of his projected work upon *Lourdes* were not perhaps so naïve in making him so welcome at the famous grotto; if Huysmans could come over, why not Zola? But they reckoned, perhaps, without Zola's clarity, his lack of complexity. In the days of his misery it might perhaps have happened, but if his new-found happiness had made him anxious to find an Utopia which could give all men freedom and life without struggle, it had not made him prepared to accept the waste of the *status quo* as the price of his new faith. It was, of course, exactly the individual belief of the faithful, the priests and the nuns who tended the sick which he celebrated in

Lourdes (1894), exactly the Church's organization of the grotto, the payments which were so important a source of revenue for the Church's work, which he attacked so violently. A naïve response – even more naïve, perhaps, his surprise that the Church was not pleased – but exactly this naïveté kept his vision of social injustice so clear, his Socialism intact.

As a work of art, *Lourdes* has much of Zola at his best in it. The train packed with hideously diseased people, the agony of the jolting, the stifling heat, the devoted nuns and priests, the vital faith that makes the singing of the Offices an intense happiness despite the horror around – all this is unforgettable. The brilliance of these opening chapters is unfortunately swallowed up in scattered action, meaningless detail, and melodrama that is too little prepared to be convincing. Already one feels that mechanical atmosphere of the writer who is too tired to make his vision coherent, who cannot find energy to force the scattered elements into a whole.

All this is but too apparent in *Rome* (1896), an attack upon Leo XIII's Catholic Action as a deceptive reformist mask for reactionary politics. The visit of Émile and Alexandrine to Italy was a royal progress, but although they were richly entertained in royal circles, they were not, of course, received by the Pope. One is only amazed at the simplicity that led Zola to suppose the Pope would wish to see the author of *Lourdes*, or that intimacy with the outlawed Royal family was the road to the Vatican. But if the tour produced a novel that is reminiscent of Rafael Sabatini in its improbable atmosphere of intrigue and poisoning, it gave Zola great personal pleasure in making acquaintance with his father's family in Northern Italy.

Paris (1898), the last of the *Trois Cités*, is a better work. It is largely a novel à clef of the famous Parisians of the day, and shows the growing interest which Zola was feeling for the political theories and personalities of his time. The happy solution, however, is hardly adequate to the brilliant analysis. L'Abbé Froment, whose faith had been shaken by Lourdes and broken by his failure to win Leo XIII's approval of his scheme for a new Socialist church, renounces his orders and finds happiness in a fertile union unblessed by any ceremony.

While *Paris* was still appearing in serial form, however, Zola's happy bliss was to be broken by the revelations of a provincial lawyer. It was in the autumn of 1897 that Louis Leblois showed to Zola the documents left to him by Colonel Picquart before his banishment. They made it perfectly clear that Dreyfus who had been suffering on Devil's Island since 1894 was innocent, and that Picquart himself had only been removed from the scene because he had stumbled on a truth which the General Staff so desperately needed to hide. They also made clear that the real spy, who had tried to sell France's military secrets to Germany, was Esterhazy, the dashing social figure, and not the Jewish Dreyfus, whilst if they confused some of the names, they revealed the complicity of high-up war office authorities. Zola's reaction was immediate and courageous. Although he had not before considered the details of the Dreyfus case clearly, Léon Daudet tells us that he had already expressed doubt about the findings of the 1894 trial. In any case, the enemies he was to fight were old ones: the military staff who had shouted abuse at *La Débâcle*, the Church that had put *Lourdes* on the Index. Nor was the Jewish cause a new one to him; already his alarm at growing anti-semitism in powerful circles had caused him to publish

Pour les Juifs in *Figaro* for 16th May, 1896. Now in the
same paper he expressed his admiration for the Pro-
testant deputy, Scheurer-Kestner, who had espoused
Dreyfus' cause. *Figaro's* readers would stand no more,
so that Zola was forced to publish his own pamphlets –
La Lettre à la Jeunesse addressed to the students, which
brought him the support of the young Proust, and *La
Lettre à la France,* addressed to the nation. The rigged-up
trial and acquittal of Esterhazy, however, threatened
to put an end to the campaign for the revision of Dreyfus'
sentence. Only a dramatic stroke could keep the re-
visionist cause alive and it was exactly this which Zola
provided.

The flair for journalism and self-advertisement which
Flaubert had so disliked in the old days was now to serve
a wider cause. On 13th January, 1898, *L'Aurore* published an article entitled *J'Accuse* and signed by Émile
Zola. Addressed to Félix Faure, the President of France,
it demanded Dreyfus' retrial, and accused various witnesses at the trial of 1894 with deliberate intent to foil
justice. Three hundred thousand copies were sold the
same day. The interest of the whole nation was focused
upon Zola's charges. The outcry from the Right forced
an unwilling Government to take action, though the
military authorities insisted that attention should be confined to as small an issue as possible. As a result Zola was
tried for libel against the handwriting experts, whose
declaration, that they had recognized Dreyfus' writing
in the famous scraps of papers, he had attacked as
knowingly false. With a shouting mob round the law
courts, a hostile press publishing the names of the jurors
with veiled threats, Zola's condemnation was a fore-
gone conclusion. None of his witnesses were allowed to
finish their evidence, but his own courageous speech

could not be prevented. He was fined three thousand francs and condemned to a year's imprisonment. On appeal the verdict was annulled on legal grounds. However, the case was re-opened amidst such hostile crowds, that Zola's counsel persuaded him much against his will to flee the country.

On 19th July, 1898, he landed secretly in England. Both he and Madame Zola protested against this flight, preferring imprisonment to exile. However we may view his flight, Zola had already done what was required by exposing in the fullest public glare at home and abroad the fears and lies of the Military Staff. The conspiracy of silence that had followed Dreyfus' trial was broken and a war of nerves followed in which the guilty parties inevitably broke down.

Zola's exile in England was naturally not very happy, though two visits from Jeanne and his children and one from Alexandrine broke his solitude. He was an incongruous figure to be isolated in the private hotels of Norwood, Weybridge and Sydenham. He knew no English and disliked the food intensely. However, he bicycled about the countryside with his professorial beard, pincenez and knickerbockers, and became very attached to it. At first the events of 1898 left him too shaken to do more than read Stendhal. He then made a serious study of the works of Fourier, whose ideas shaped the message of his last books. He could not remain long, however, without writing. Through the tedium, then, of the wet Victorian Sundays of the winter of 1898–9, with the Sydenham Salvation Army performing outside his window, and the prospect of the hotel high tea before him, he wrote *Fécondité*. It is tempting to think that something of those rainy streets and soggy suet puddings are to blame for the dreariness of that novel which was completed in May

1899. By 5th June, 1899, Dreyfus' condemnation was annulled and Zola returned to France.

Les Quatres Évangiles, of which only three were written, occupied the rest of Zola's life. *Fécondité, Travail, Vérité*: the names speak for the books. They show the redemption of the world through the descendants of Abbé Froment, the hero of *Les Trois Cités*. *Fécondité*, the story of Matthieu Froment, is a paean of praise to domestic fertility, with a never-ending line of fine, handsome, strong young men with forward gazes, and sweet, healthy, happy young girls with gentle, busy fingers like some great panel of a 1912 Town Hall representing Industry and the Arts. In *Travail* we are given the Fourierist organization of society with its busy, happy phalansteries, teeming like bee-hives or ant-mounds. *Vérité* retells the injustice of the Dreyfus case, with the curious theme of a pederastic rape and murder, and the eventual triumph of lay education when the crime is brought home to a priest. It is difficult not to treat these last novels with ridicule, for they are so lifeless and solemn. The theme of a Socialist Utopia can, of course, be made the source of very real literary inspiration, as in Morris's *News from Nowhere*, but for Zola such a theme, one must suspect, was an escape from recognition of the social injustice and corruption which he knew to be no less real than when he had written *L'Assommoir*. In the last resort one can only rejoice that his own life had acquired the tranquillity and happiness that made him turn aside in this way, and, remembering the greatness of his best work and the courage of his defence of Dreyfus, we may excuse though we need not read the lapses of his last years.

The end, when it came, was strange and sudden. On 28th September, 1902, an early cold spell decided the

Zolas to leave Médan for their Paris home. A fire was burning in their bedroom to welcome their return. As usual they slept without open windows. The chimney, however, had become blocked during the summer, and in the middle of the night, the couple awoke, choking from charcoal fumes. Émile got out of bed and fell to the floor. Alexandrine, who remained in bed, was insensible, though still alive in the morning; but Zola, despite two hours of artificial respiration, died at ten in the morning. The homage that greeted the news of his death was world-wide; and Anatole France, who spoke the funeral oration, voiced the feelings of the thousands of Zola's readers and of the millions of his political admirers, when he declared, 'He was a moment of human conscience.'

Appendix

ZOLA AND HIS ENGLISH AND AMERICAN READERS*

A short statement upon the reception of Émile Zola's novels in England and the United States seems desirable, not only for the intrinsic interest which the subject may be supposed to have for Anglo-Saxon readers, but also because it can shed some light upon the near oblivion into which his work has fallen in countries, where on many grounds it might have been expected to enjoy considerable popularity.

The licence of Zola's treatment of sexual subjects defied the great prohibition which dominated Victorian literature and was sufficient to outlaw his work in other than mangled form from a reading public whose greatest allegiance was given to Dickens. Yet in its imaginative sources, its broad social canvas, its creation of a supposedly realistic world to convey a nightmare vision, the Rougon-Macquart country is the next-door kingdom to the land where the fog lies thick around the Chancery Court and Rogue Riderhood scours the muddy river for bodies. In that curious combination of prurience, sexuality and Puritan horror which we now may guess to have thrilled Victorian readers as they followed Quilp's pursuit of Little Nell or Bradley Headstone's manic desire for Lizzie Hexham, Zola far outstripped Charles Dickens. Zola's attack upon contemporary society was no more fierce than that of Dickens, but the pill was not sugared.

* This Appendix refers, of course, to general readers. Zola's work has never been entirely without its admirers in academical circles in both countries.

In the purely emotional and moral source of his work, in
the lack of abstraction or intellectualism of all the greater
of his novels, Zola was more in key with the English
tradition than with that of his own country. Indeed it
may be said that where he fails to be universal, his moral
order is in many respects far more Anglo-Saxon than
French. Nevertheless his direct approach to sexual subjects doomed his work from the start in contemporary
England or America. By the time that a more liberal
climate obtained, and it must be said that even today
many of the descriptions in *La Terre* would evoke comment if they appeared in a newly published novel, the
general forms of his novels and the nineteenth-century
ethos of his materialism had put him out of fashion. In
his frankness of speech he was decades ahead of Victorian
England, in the 'modernity' of his theories, so inessen-
tial to his work and so essential to his amour-propre,
he was already dowdy some time before his death. For
the great reading public, then, he was consigned to the
secret drawer of 'dirty' books or ranged high on the
dusty shelves of 'outdated classics'. Except for the
strictly limited readers who subscribed to the Lutetian
edition, his novels were available only after they had been
suitably cut by earnest but prudish social reformers, or
no less distortingly headlined and advertised by publishers with an eye on the sensational market. The history
of this process is as interesting a commentary upon the
superficiality of changing literary judgment as it is upon
the tyranny of public morality.

Zola's name had been damned in England before any
of his works appeared in translation. If the publication
of *L'Assommoir* in 1877 met with some outcries from
Radicals in France for its portrayal of slum morality,
there was little that could equal Swinburne's attack in the

Athenaeum entitled 'A Note on the Question of the Hour.' It is not altogether surprising to find the secret author of *The Whippingham Papers* declaiming against 'such details of brutality and atrocity practised on a little girl, as would necessitate the interpolation of such a line as follows in the police report of any and every newspaper in London: ''The further details given in support of the charge of cruelty were too revolting for publication in our columns''.' A reviewer in the *Gentleman's Magazine* for December 1878 paid *L'Assommoir* high praise. 'The book will live', he wrote, 'and work. It is powerful and terrible.' But even this admirer felt it necessary to give warning of Zola's frank tone, which he attempted to excuse with an explanation of the differences of French and English taste – 'The English authors will not leave a celestial bed to prey on garbage. French writers sometimes do not shun even ordure.' This was not, perhaps, a happy augury for any would-be translator. Andrew Lang attempted a serious if somewhat neutral review of Zola's work in the *Fortnightly Review* in 1882. But the publication of *Pot-Bouille* in 1883, which so angered French bourgeois critics, had its repercussions in England where the *Scottish Review* declared 'It is certainly coarse almost beyond reproduction, and contains one description which should never have been written by man born of woman.' As yet, however, no translation had appeared in England.

The absence of copyright safeguards created a very different situation in the United States. There was little to prevent the moulding of Zola's work to satisfy the public curiosity without disturbing the public sense of decency. Henry James, whose early and somewhat unfavourable impressions of Zola were later to be so strikingly reversed, had already given some warning to his fellow countrymen in an article sent from Europe to the *New York Tribune* in 1876. 'Émile Zola,' he wrote, 'a pupil of Gustave Flaubert's, is a novelist the most thoroughgoing of the little band of out-and-out realists. Unfortunately the real for him means exclusively the unclean, and he utters his crudities with an air of bravado which makes them doubly intolerable.' Henry James in his earliest meetings with Zola had received only the impression of his arrogance and was undoubtedly hostile. Later meetings were so to alter his view that after a discussion with Zola on the vocabulary of *L'Assommoir*, he was chiefly struck by his immense modesty. As James' own work developed, so did his appreciation of Zola; at the time of his work on *The Princess Casamassima* (1884) he wrote very appreciatively to Howells of *La Joie de Vivre*. But it was not until long after Zola's death that the famous panegyric appeared in the *Atlantic Monthly* of August 1913. Whatever the young Henry James' fears of Zola's crudities in 1876, the enterprising Philadelphia firm of publishers Messrs. Peterson felt safe in producing a translation of *Une Page d'Amour* in 1878, entitled 'Hélène. A love episode.' Their choice, of course, was discreet. The translation was by Mary Neale Sherwood, who was to undertake translations of most of the Rougon-Macquart series for the same publishers. In 1879 however, when *L'Assommoir* was produced, she assumed the name of John Stirling, and retained this more suitable masculine pseudonym for all her subsequent translations, including a reissue of *Hélène* in 1882, now more attractively subtitled 'A tale of love and passion.' There was little to fear, perhaps, from the impact of her version of *L'Assommoir* upon the public, for she had avowedly 'toned down with literary ability, combined with tact, delicacy and refinement to suit the American reading public.' What was not made so clear was that in so doing she had reduced Zola's novel by half. The standard of translation, too, was low, poorer in fact than that which Vizetelly was to present to the English public. What was lacking in authenticity, however, was made up for by the exciting slant given to Zola's work by the titles. A few examples will suffice to show the approach – a combination of 'daring', 'Gay Paree', and 'the eternal feminine' of the Anglo-Saxon's dream view of France: – 'Albine, or The Abbé's Temptation' (*La Faute de l'Abbé Mouret*), 'La Belle Lisa, or the Paris Market girls' (*Le Ventre de Paris*), 'Christine the Model, or Studies of Love' (*L'Œuvre*), 'The Devil's Compact' (*Thérèse Raquin*), 'Mysteries of the Court of Louis Napoleon' (*Son Excellence*), 'Wedded in Death' (*La Fortune des Rougon*), 'A Woman's Heart' (*Une Page d'Amour*), 'A terrible confession, or the sufferings of a lost soul in a garret' (*La Confession de Claude*). But Petersons were not the only publishers, nor Mary Neale Sherwood the only translator in the field. Mr. Salvan in a very interesting article on the subject published in *Brown University Studies* states that between 1878 and 1900 thirty-one publishers produced one hundred and eighty editions of Zola's novels. After the Dreyfus case, it is true, American liberal opinion like English began to see Zola as a great moral figure; as a result more reputable translations began to appear, including Macmillan's editions of the authorized Vizetelly translations, which, however poor, were at least unabridged, though only then of the more 'safe novels'. But the avalanche of sensationalism was enough to bury Zola's greatness, and something of this approach has persisted even today. A recent reprint of 'Piping Hot. By Émile Zola, author of *Nana*' contains the following typical 'blurb'. 'THE

BOOK THAT MADE ALL PARIS GASP! Piping Hot! That's what Émile Zola himself called this remarkable book. More daring than *Nana*, more sizzling than a dozen of the great French romances, it is truly an exciting reading experience. Drawn with burning accuracy from the romances and bedroom intrigues of a single building in Zola's Paris, here is a novel that will fascinate the most exacting with its women of secret passions and its men of hidden lusts . . . When youthful Octave Meuret (sic) comes to Paris from the country, he is inexperienced, provincial. Yet very rapidly the young man discovers the backstairs route that leads to carnal love. With Berthe, his neighbour's wife, Octave rises to the heights of passion, until the shattering of their midnight tryst rocks the house like an earthquake. With Madame Hedouin, he tries to mix pleasure with business and lands on the red side of Cupid's ledger. . . . With the men of the house, the husbands and bachelors, Octave learns all there is to know of the night life of Paris, of the Paris of kept women, amorous rendezvous, and back door intrigues.' It is perhaps not altogether surprising that the reviewer of *The Critic* for 1883 declared — 'like his predecessor, the Marquis de Sade, Zola seems to be following the path which leads to madness.' Though the same critic was one of the first to remark on the doubtful, 'Pamela-like' morality of *Au Bonheur des Dames*, pointing out that the only possible conclusion was that if a pretty shopgirl flirted adroitly enough with her employer, she would become the patronne.

The first British translation of a Zola novel did not appear until seven years after Mary Sherwood's *Hélène*. In 1885 the Vizetelly family, who had launched their publishing firm five years before, produced a translation of *L'Assommoir*, followed shortly afterwards by *Nana*. It cannot be said that the atmosphere was exactly propitious, for W. S. Lilly in an article in *The Fortnightly Review* entitled 'The New Naturalism' wrote: 'The New Naturalism eliminates from men all but the ape and the tiger . . . it is a victory of fact over principle, of mechanism over imagination, of appetites dignified as rights over duties, of sensation over intellect.' The Vizetelly enterprise was therefore all the more courageous and commendable. They issued the works whole, they respected the writer's high intention and revered him as an artist. Neither Henry Vizetelly, the father, nor Ernest Vizetelly, the son, were unfortunately particularly suited to grasp the scope or nature of Zola's novels. Energetic, high-minded radicals with their background of London Radical Bohemia, their journalistic experiences in Paris of the Commune, their enterprises in typography, engraving and publishing intended to bring learning within the scope of the artisan classes, they command respect which cannot but be tempered with amusement. They seem at once to hark back to the middle-class radicalism of Hone and Holcroft and Godwin, and forward to the suburban radicalism of early Wells. Ernest Vizetelly, who by his loyalty and assistance to Zola became the sole authorized English translator of the novels, has left many reminiscences which give us some idea of the limited scope of his understanding of his hero. Of Zola's early attachment to the Paris prostitute, which forms the theme of *La Confession de Claude*, he remarks: 'We know to what a young man's fancy turns in springtime, and Zola was as human as others.'

Later when Zola was exiled in Norwood, Vizetelly found his melancholy difficult to understand – 'taking his meals in private and holding no intercourse with his neighbours, his loneliness increased, though Norwood around him was teeming with life.' When Zola in 1887 gave up wine with his meals in order to reduce his weight, his English disciple comments 'so it will be seen that he was almost a total abstainer.' Though his approach to his own work as translator was disarmingly modest, for he confessed that most of it was of poor quality over-hurriedly performed to meet debts or the demands of publishers who cared about novelty rather than quality, Vizetelly cannot be said to have had much more grasp of the scope of Zola's novels than of the novelist himself. 'From a purely literary point of view', he says, 'Germinal is superior to L'Assommoir, because it contains less slang.' If La Terre seems too black in its portrayal of humanity, he declares, 'in Nana the general blackness of the characters does not seem out of place, for only men and women of a sorry sort gravitate round a harlot. As regards L'Assommoir respecting which the author has often cordially re-echoed the opinion that it is one of the greatest temperance tracts ever written, one can only say that, like other books of Zola's, it has done good in individual instances, but has failed to stem the general passion for strong drink.' This aspect of Zola's work apparently made great appeal to him, for again he tells us: 'It would not appear that the flagellation of vice which one finds in the Rougon-Macquart novels has had any widespread effect in France, though it has undoubtedly done good in individual cases.'

Such was the man, then, whose honest, if inadequate translations first presented Zola's novels to the English reading public. It was not until 1888, however, that the storm of outraged morality broke over the Vizetellys. In that year they published a translation of La Terre. Ernest himself had been worried about the coarseness

of language and insisted on altering Hyacinthe's sob-
riquet of Jésus Christ and omitting the farting match.
These were insufficient precautions. W. T. Stead was
watchful as ever over the concerns of public morality
in *The Pall Mall Gazette*, and the National Vigilance
Association quickly followed suit. A motion was put
forward in the House. The Government was unwilling
to take action, but eventually a private prosecution was
arranged. Henry Vizetelly was charged with having published three obscene books – *Nana*, *Pot-Bouille* and *La
Terre*. Sir Edward Clarke read extracts in a broad English
accent; when he came to the passage in *La Terre* of the
mating of the bull, the horrified jury requested him to
stop. Henry Vizetelly was fined £100. Unfortunately
monetary pressure on the firm made them risk further
translations both of Zola and of Maupassant. The old man
was again committed for trial, the firm went into liquid-
ation and Henry Vizetelly to prison for three months.

This triumph for public morality put a stop to any
serious undertaking of the translation of Zola's work into
English. As Puritanism and lack of copyright had consigned his work to sensational publication in the United
States, so Puritanism and the English law handed it over
to the tract vendors. Charles Reade's dramatization of
L'Assommoir was the only serious approach for the next
ten years. For the rest Zola's novels were boiled down
into twenty-page tracts of which 'Gervaise Coupeau.
A story of drink' is a good example. The travesty of
Zola's work may be judged from the following passage
with which the work ends. Gervaise, widowed after
the drunken death of Coupeau, is reformed and married
to Goujet. Dear little Nana, a saved child, sits beside
them. 'May mamma have some of this dish, Papa Goujet?' said Nana. 'And then, me, a little. I am *so* hungry,

but don't give her any wine – no wine, papa, for my other papa was killed by wine.' 'I'll try to live again!' said Gervaise. 'And a happy life this time', Goujet added, 'for Drink *shall* not enter our home.'

In 1891, it is true, Chatto and Windus agreed to take Vizetelly's translation of *La Débâcle*, and thereafter the later novels were given to the public in somewhat hurried but fairly complete translations. Macmillan also published these translations in the United States.

In 1893 Zola visited England with his wife in order to address the Institute of Journalists. The considerable reception he received showed that even if public morality prevented his works being available to less educated readers, the literary world at last recognized his importance. A dinner was arranged at the Authors' Club, Sir Walter Besant presiding. He was made an honorary member of the Athenaeum for the length of his visit. A civic reception was held at the Guildhall. Dr. Garnett showed him round the British Museum. He mistook matins at Westminster Abbey for high mass and was surprised that the church should still be Catholic. He visited Oxford in the rain. It was Vizetelly who made all the arrangements as he did for Zola's year-long exile here in 1898–9. It was perhaps only just that so long as no more complete and adequate translations than Vizetelly's could appear, his devotion should have been rewarded by Zola's trust, but his translations are not the less inadequate.

The barrier put up by the results of the Vizetelly case is the more pathetic when it is considered that translations of the Rougon-Macquart novels have in fact been made by some of the most outstanding literary men of the late nineteenth century. The whole series was published for private circulation only by the Lutetian Society in 1894–5. Havelock Ellis translated *Germinal*, Arthur Symons *L'Assommoir*, Ernest Dowson *La Terre*. Of these only *Germinal* has been reprinted in a general edition here and in the United States. By the time that a great latitude of language was permissible in the novel, critical opinion had dismissed Zola's work with the general holocaust of the nineteenth century that set in after 1914. Henry James' great eulogy in 1913 came too late, and no one, except V. S. Pritchett, and Josephson, has written seriously about Zola in English since that date. Recent translations of *Nana* in the United States and Thomas Walton's translation of *L'Œuvre* suggest that a change in attitude may be imminent.

BIBLIOGRAPHICAL GUIDE TO THE
LITERARY WORK OF ZOLA

Published by Lacroix:

Contes à Ninon. 1864
La Confession de Claude. 1866
Mes Haines. 1866
Le Vœu d'une Morte. 1866
Les Mystères de Marseille. 1866
Thérèse Raquin. 1868
Madeleine Férat. 1868
La Fortune des Rougon. 1871

Published by Charpentier (following the bankruptcy
of Lacroix):

La Curée. 1872
Le Ventre de Paris. 1873
La Conquête de Plassans. 1874
La Faute de l'Abbé Mouret. 1875
Son Excellence Eugène Rougon. 1876
L'Assommoir. 1877
Une Page d'Amour. 1878
La République et la Littérature. 1879
Le Roman Expérimental. 1880
Nana. 1880
Nos Auteurs Dramatiques. 1881
Les Romanciers Naturalistes. 1881
Pot-Bouille. 1882
Une Campagne. 1882
Au Bonheur des Dames. 1883

Published by Charpentier—*contd.*

La Joie de Vivre. 1884

Germinal. 1885

L'Œuvre. 1886

La Terre. 1887

Le Rêve. 1888

Le Naturalisme au Théâtre. 1889

La Bête Humaine. 1890

L'Argent. 1891

La Débâcle. 1892

Le Docteur Pascal. 1893

Lourdes. 1894

La Nouvelle Campagne. 1896

Rome. 1896

Paris. 1898

Fécondité. 1899

Travail. 1901

Vérité. 1902

The main French edition of Zola's works, edited with prefaces by his son-in-law and disciple Maurice Le Blond, is a remarkably good production. Each novel contains selections from Zola's working notes as an appendix. The edition was published by François Bernouard (1927–9). The manuscripts of all the Rougon-Macquart series save one, which is in the United States, are at the Bibiothèque Nationale, as are all his working notes.

TRANSLATIONS IN ENGLAND

Henry and Ernest Vizetelly published all the Rougon-Macquart series up to *La Terre* in translation, except *Au Bonheur des Dames* which was translated by F. Belmont

and published by Tinsley in 1883. The Vizetelly enterprise began in 1884 with the publication of *L'Assommoir*
and ended with the disastrous publication of *La Terre* as
'Soil' in 1888. Edmondo de Amicis contributed a preface to *l'Assommoir* in which he stressed the moral value
of Zola's work. George Moore contributed prefaces to
'The Rush for the Spoil' (*La Curée*) and 'Piping Hot'
(*Pot-Bouille*), laying emphasis on Zola as the *poet* of
realism. Translations of the Rougon-Macquart series
began again with Ernest Vizetelly's 'The Downfall' (*La
Débâcle*) in 1892, published by Chatto & Windus. All
Zola's novels subsequent to *La Débâcle* were translated
by Ernest Vizetelly and published by Chatto & Windus.
A number of the earlier Rougon-Macquart novels were
re-edited by Ernest Vizetelly from the translations
originally published by his father. Most of the titles
were altered to appeal to popular taste, and Vizetelly
felt compelled not only to bowdlerize the text but to
alter and rearrange certain incidents to satisfy public
morality. Most of these bowdlerized versions were published by Chatto & Windus, though some were issued
by Hutchinson, and *Thérèse Raquin* was not republished
until the 1902 edition produced by Grant Richards.
L'Assommoir which was now called 'The Dramshop' (1894)
was the most altered. Neither *La Terre* nor *Nana* was published in this new enterprise. *Le Rêve* alone of the Rougon-
Macquart series, though published by Chatto & Windus,
was not translated by Vizetelly but by Eliza Chase. The
only novel of the series, no doubt, that seemed suitable
for a woman's care. A translation of *Nana* was published
by Cecil Palmer in 1926. Apart from the Lutetian Society
publications, the only other translation of a novel of
Zola since Vizetelly's day is Mr. Thomas Walton's excellent 'The Masterpiece', published by Paul Elek in

1950. In 1894 and 1895 the Lutetian Society issued *complete* translations of six of the Rougon-Macquart novels in three hundred copies each. The translators were men of outstanding literary position:

Nana	translated by	V. Plarr.
L'Assommoir	,,	A. Symons
Pot-Bouille	,,	Percy Pinkerton.
La Curée	,,	A. Teixeira de Mattos.
La Terre	,,	Ernest Dowson.
Germinal	,,	Havelock Ellis.

Havelock Ellis' *Germinal* was reissued by Dent in the Everyman Series in 1933. Symons' *L'Assommoir* was reissued for private circulation by Werner Laurie in 1928.

The Lutetian Society series were officially approved by Zola, quite unabridged and of a far higher standard than any other translations. They are by no means satisfactory, however, in conveying either the energy or visual impressionism of Zola's style.

'The Attack on the Mill', a collection of Zola's short stories, was published by Heinemann in 1892, with an essay by Edmund Gosse. The essay is, like so much of his writing, an interesting light on Gosse's outlook rather than a contribution to the study of Zola.

TRANSLATIONS IN THE UNITED STATES

The novels of the Rougon-Macquart series down to *Au Bonheur des Dames* were published between 1878 and 1882 by Peterson of Philadelphia. The translations were made by Mary Sherwood, all except *Une Page d'Amour* under the pseudonym of John Stirling. They are more readable versions than those of Vizetelly, but less exact in language and more abridged. Peterson also published *La Terre*, *La Bête Humaine* and *L'Œuvre* translated by G. D. Cox. Many of Vizetelly's translations were published in the United States by Macmillan. A considerable number of Zola's novels translated by various persons were issued from American publishing houses in the late nineteenth and early twentieth centuries. In 1924 Boni & Liveright published the Lutetian Society series. Knopf, like Dent, published Havelock Ellis' translation of *Germinal*. In general, translations of a higher standard have been published since the end of the First World War. These include a translation of *L'Assommoir* with an introduction by Havelock Ellis (Knopf, 1924), *Germinal* with an introduction by Josephson (Knopf, 1937), *La Bête Humaine*, a limited edition (Julian Press, Newark, 1932), *L'Œuvre* translated by Katherine Woods (Howell, Soskin, 1946), and five different versions of *Nana* from publishers of good standing.

WORKS ON ZOLA

In so far as Zola's novels require information outside their own covers to assist in their interpretation, the most important source lies in his letters published in two volumes, *Lettres de Jeunesse* and *Les Lettres et les Arts*. Any critic who, like myself, adopts a partly Freudian interpretation will find particular interest in the first of the two volumes. For contemporary evaluation of his work and personality, the two most interesting sources are, of course, the letters of Flaubert and the Goncourt Journals. Léon Daudet's *Souvenirs* are both spiteful and illuminating. Two aspects of hostile contemporary literary criticism may be found in Brunetière's *Le Roman*

Naturaliste (1883) and Barbey D'Aurévilley's *Les Œuvres et les Hommes* (1902). Anatole France's views at the date of publication – he is never predictable – are in *La Vie Littéraire* (1889). An academic view as appreciative as Brunetière is hostile is Lemaître's *Contemporains* (1888). The earliest biography is that by his great friend Paul Alexis (1882), who published Zola's early poems with this appreciation. A tribute by the chief of the disciples of Zola's later life is Maurice Le Blond's *Zola devant les Jeunes* (1898). Important also are *Le Roman Naturaliste sous le Second Empire* (1913) and *Naturalisme Français* (1923), by Pierre Martino. Various contributions by later followers may be found in the *Bulletin de l'Association Émile Zola*. Perhaps the most interesting earlier account of Zola's work is contained in *Comment Émile Zola composait ses Romans* (1906), a remarkable work by Massis, then a very young man.

Of foreign contemporaries who wrote on Zola, the most important are:

Henry James, whose growing appreciation may be traced in his letters and reviews, culminating in the essay contained in *Notes on Novelists* (1913).

Georg Brandes has an essay on Zola in his *Moderne Geister* (1889). His estimate is based only upon the earlier novels of the Rougon-Macquart series, but, with this limitation, it is, as might be expected, very penetrating and is, perhaps, the earliest appreciation of the 'black poet' aspect of Zola.

Turgenev's comments upon Zola's work have perhaps only the interest attaching to his association with the Flaubert circle.

Tolstoy's view is contained in *Zola, Dumas, Maupassant* (1896).

The account of Zola's approach to his work given by

Edmondo de Amicis, the result of a long interview, is of primary importance. It appears in *Souvenirs de Paris et de Londres* (1880). It has additional importance in view of the great contemporary popularity of Zola's work, especially in dramatized form, in Italy.

The interest of the views of Heinrich Mann, in his *Geist und Tat* (1931), lies chiefly in Zola's great influence on his early work in such novels as *Der Untertan* and *Schlaraffenland*.

Jules Romains' views in *Zola et son Exemple* (1935) have largely the same value.

Sherard's work, published in 1897, and Ernest Vizetelly's, in 1904, give two different favourable approaches in contemporary England.

Vollard's *Cézanne* (1912) is, of course, the chief statement of the case against Zola in his relations with the painter.

The official biography of Zola is the short study by his daughter Denise Le Blond-Zola, published in 1931. She gives an interesting picture both of her mother and of Madame Émile Zola.

Henri Barbusse's life, published in 1932, is that of a great admirer, who regrets Zola's failure to develop into a full Marxist. The English translation by Mary and F. C. Green was published by Dent in the same year. A more modern Marxist view, commented on in the text of this book, is contained in Lukacs' *Studies in European Realism*. (English edition. Hillway Publishing Co. 1950.)

The only considerable book on Zola in English is Matthew Josephson's *Zola and his Time* (U.S. edition (1928), English edition (1929)). It is a large, sprawling book, written in a curiously rhapsodical style, and containing no references. But there are many estimates of great value in it, and the author does get near to seeing the importance of the personal element in Zola's work.

A Zola Dictionary: with a Biographical and Critical Introduction, Synopses of the Plots of the Rougon-Macquart Novels, and a Bibliographical Note, by J. G. Patterson (Routledge, 1912), is a thorough and useful compendium.

Among many articles in learned periodicals, two perhaps have especial interest for English and American readers. Salvan: *Zola aux États-Unis* (Brown University Studies) and Decker: *Zola's literary reputation in England* (Proceedings of the Modern Language Association, vol. XLIX, 1934).

APOLLO EDITIONS